# ARKANSAS NARRATIVES

# *The WPA Arkansas Slave Narratives Collection:*

## *A Folk History of Slavery in the United States from Interviews with Former Slaves*

# PART 7

**TYPEWRITTEN RECORDS PREPARED BY
THE FEDERAL WRITERS' PROJECT
1936-1938
ASSEMBLED BY
THE LIBRARY OF CONGRESS PROJECT
WORK PROJECTS ADMINISTRATION
FOR THE DISTRICT OF COLUMBIA
SPONSORED BY THE LIBRARY OF CONGRESS**

WASHINGTON 1941

Prepared by
the Federal Writers' Project of
the Works Progress Administration
for the State of Florida

# ARKANSAS NARRATIVES

# PREPARED FOR PUBLICATION
# BY
# HISTORIC PUBLISHING SERIES™

*Slave Narratives: A Folk History of Slavery in the United States*
*From Interviews with Former Slaves*

# HISTORIC PUBLISHING
SAN ANTONIO, TEXAS
©2017 All Rights Reserved
*Slavery Books & African American History Courses & Resources*
https://africanamericanhistorybooks.blogspot.com

# ARKANSAS NARRATIVES

# INFORMANTS

1. Interviewer: Irene Robertson Subject: NEGRO LORE Story:— Information This information given by: Charlie Vaden Place of Residence: Hazen, Green Grove, Ark. Occupation: Farming Age: 77

2. Interviewer: Miss Irene Robertson Person interviewed: Ellen Vaden DeValls Bluff, Ark. Age: 83

3. Interviewer: Miss Irene Robertson Person interviewed: Nettie Van Buren, Clarendon, Arkansas Ex school-teacher Age: 62

4. Name of Interviewer: Samuel S. Taylor Person Interviewed: Adelaide J. Vaughn 1122 Cross Street, Little Rock, Arkansas Age: 69

5. Interviewer: Mrs. Blanche Edwards Person interviewed: Emmeline Waddille (deceased) Lonoke County, Arkansas Age: 106

6. STATE—Arkansas NAME OF WORKER—Blanche Edwards ADDRESS—Lonoke, Arkansas DATE—October 20, 1938 SUBJECT—An Old Slave

7. Interviewer: Samuel S. Taylor Person interviewed: Henry Waldon 816 Walnut Street. North Little Rock, Arkansas Age: 84

8. Interviewer: Mary D. Hudgins Person interviewed: Aunt Clara Walker Aged: 111 Home: "Flatwoods" district, Garland County. Own property.

9. Interviewer: Miss Irene Robertson Person interviewed: Henry Walker, Hazen, Arkansas Age: 80

10. Interviewer: Irene Robertson Subject: Ex-Slave-Hunting Story:— Information This information given by: Henry Walker Place of Residence: Hazen, Arkansas Occupation: Farmer. Age: 78

11. Interviewer: Mrs. Bernice Bowden Person interviewed: Jake Walker 3002 Short W. Ninth Avenue, Pine Bluff, Arkansas Age: 95

12. Interviewer: Miss Irene Robertson Person interviewed: Jake Walker, Wheatley, Arkansas Age: 68

13. Interviewer: Bernice Bowden Person interviewed: Willie Wallace 40th and Georgia Streets, Pine Bluff, Arkansas Age: 80

14. Interviewer: Mrs. Bernice Bowden Person interviewed: Evans Warrior 609 E. 23rd Avenue, Pine Bluff, Arkansas Age: 80

15. Interviewer: Miss Irene Robertson Person interviewed: Anna Washington, Clarendon, Arkansas (Back of Mrs. Maynard's home in the alley) Age: 77

16. FOLKLORE SUBJECTS Interviewer: S.S. Taylor Subject: Slave memories—Birth, Mother, Father, Separation House Subject: Slaves—Dwellings, Food, Clothes Subject: Corn Shucking, Dances, Quiltings, Weddings among Slaves Subject: Slaves—Fight with Master (junior); Slave uprisings Subject: Confederate Army Negroes; Ex-slave Occupations Story:—Information This information given by: Eliza Washington Place of Residence: 1517 West Seventeenth Little Rock, Arkansas Occupation: Washing and Ironing (When able) Age: About 77

17. Interviewer: Miss Irene Robertson Person interviewed: Jennie Washington, DeValls Bluff, Arkansas Age: 80

18. Interviewer: Mrs. Bernice Bowden Person interviewed: Parrish Washington 812 Spruce Street, Pine Bluff, Arkansas Age: 86

19. Interviewer: Mrs. Bernice Bowden Person interviewed: Caroline Watson 517 E. 21st Avenue, Pine Bluff, Arkansas Age: 82

20. STATE—Arkansas NAME OF WORKER—Samuel S. Taylor ADDRESS—Little Rock, Arkansas DATE—December, 1938 SUBJECT—Ex-slave

21. Interviewer: Miss Irene Robertson Person interviewed: Person interviewed: Bart Wayne, Helena, Arkansas Age: 72

22. Interviewer: Pernella Anderson Person interviewed: Annie Mae Weathers East Bone Street El Dorado, Ark. Age: ?

23. Interviewer: Samuel S. Taylor Person interviewed: Cora Weathers 818 Chester Street, Little Rock, Arkansas Age: 79

24. Interviewer: Samuel S. Taylor Person interviewed: Ishe Webb 1610 Cross Street, Little Rock, Arkansas Age: 78, or more

25. Pine Bluff District FOLKLORE SUBJECTS Name of Interviewer: Martin - Barker Subject: (Negro Lore)--Ex-Slave Story:—Information This information given by: Alfred Wells Place of Residence: Occupation: Age: 77

26. Interviewer: Mrs. Bernice Bowden Person interviewed: Douglas Wells 1419 Alabama Street, Pine Bluff, Arkansas Age: 83

27. Interviewer: Miss Irene Robertson Person interviewed: John Wells, Edmondson, Arkansas Age: 82

28. Interviewer: Samuel S. Taylor Person interviewed: Sarah Wells 1012 W. Sixteenth Street, Little Rock, Arkansas Age: 84 Occupation: Field hand

29. Interviewer: Miss Irene Robertson Person interviewed: Sarah Williams Wells, Biscoe, Arkansas Age: Born 1866

30. Interviewer: Miss Irene Robertson Person interviewed: John Wesley, Helena, Arkansas Age: ?

31. Interviewer: Miss Irene Robertson Person interviewed: Robert Wesley, Holly Grove, Arkansas Age: 74

32. Interviewer: Miss Irene Robertson Person interviewed: Maggie Wesmoland, Brinkley, Arkansas Age: 85

33. Interviewer: Miss Irene Robertson Person interviewed: Calvin West, Widener, Arkansas Age: 68

34. Interviewer: Miss Irene Robertson Person interviewed: Mary Mays West, Widener, Arkansas Age: 65

35. Interviewer: Miss Irene Robertson Person interviewed: Sylvester Wethington Holly Grove, Arkansas Age: 77

36. Interviewer: Miss Irene Robertson Person interviewed: Joe Whitaker, Madison, Arkansas Age: 70 plus

37. Interviewer: Beulah Sherwood Hagg Person interviewed: Mrs. Julia A. White, 3003 Cross St., Little Rock, Ark. Age: 79

38. STATE—Arkansas NAME OF WORKER—Samuel S. Taylor ADDRESS—Little Rock, Arkansas DATE—December, 1938 SUBJECT—Ex-slave

39. Interviewer: Miss Irene Robertson Person interviewed: Lucy White, Marianna, Arkansas Age: 74

40. Interviewer: Bernice Bowden Person interviewed: David Whiteman (c) Age: 88 Home: 104 N. Kansas Street, Pine Bluff, Arkansas.

41. Interviewer: Mrs. Bernice Bowden Person interviewed: Dolly Whiteside (c) Age: 81 Home: 103 Oregon Street, Pine Bluff, Ark.

42. Interviewer: Samuel S. Taylor Person interviewed: J.W. Whitfield 3100 W. Seventeenth Street, Little Rock, Arkansas Age: About 60 Occupation: Preacher

43. Interviewer: Miss Irene Robertson Person interviewed: Sarah Whitmore, Clarendon, Arkansas Age: 100

44. Interviewer: Watt McKinney Person interviewed: Dock Wilborn A mile or so from Marvell, Arkansas Age: 95

45. Interviewer: Miss Irene Robertson Person interviewed: Bell Wilks, Holly Grove, Arkansas Age: 80

46. Interviewer: Miss Irene Robertson Person interviewed: Bell Williams, Forrest City, Arkansas Age: 85

47. Mrs. Mildred Thompson Mrs. Carol Graham El Dorado District Federal Writers Project Union County, Arkansas

48. Interviewer: Miss Irene Robertson Person interviewed: Charlie Williams Brassfield; Ark. Age: 73

49. Interviewer: Samuel S. Taylor Person interviewed: Columbus Williams Temporary: 2422 Howard Street, Little Rock, Arkansas Permanent: Box 12, Route 2, Ouachita County, Stevens, Arkansas Age: 98

50. Interviewer: Samuel S. Taylor Person interviewed: Frank Williams County Hospital, ward eleven, Little Rock, Arkansas Age: 100, or more

51. Interviewer: Thomas Elmore Lucy Person interviewed: Gus Williams, Russellville, Arkansas Age: 80

52. Interviewer: Pernella M. Anderson Person interviewed: Henrietta Williams B. Avenue, El Dorado, Arkansas Age: About 82

53. Interviewer: Miss Irene Robertson Person interviewed: Henry Andrew (Tip) Williams Biscoe, Arkansas Age: Born in 1854, 86

54. Interviewer: Miss Irene Robertson Person interviewed: James Williams, Brinkley, Arkansas Age: 72

55. Interviewer: Samuel S. Taylor Person interviewed: John Williams County Hospital, ward 11, Little Rock, Arkansas Age: 75

56. Interviewer: Miss Irene Robertson Person interviewed: Lillie Williams, Madison, Arkansas Age: 69

57. Interviewer: Miss Irene Robertson Person interviewed: Mary Williams, Clarendon, Arkansas Age: Born 1872 Light color

58. Name of Interviewer: Irene Robertson Subject: Ex-Slave—Herbs "Hant" experiences Story:—Information This information given by: Mary Williams Place of Residence: Hazen, Arkansas Occupation: Field Worker Age: 69

59. Interviewer: Mrs. Bernice Bowden Person interviewed: Mary Williams 409 North Hickory, Pine Bluff, Arkansas Age: 82

60. Interviewer: Mrs. Bernice Bowden Person interviewed: Mary Williams 409 Hickory, Pine Bluff, Arkansas Age: 84

61. Interviewer: Mrs. Bernice Bowden Person interviewed: Rosena Hunt Williams R.F.D., Brinkley, Arkansas Age: 56

62. Interviewer: Miss Irene Robertson Person interviewed: "Soldier" Williams, Forrest City, Arkansas Age: 98

63. Interviewer: Miss Irene Robertson Person interviewed: Anna Williamson, Holly Grove, Arkansas Age: Between 75 and 80

64. Interviewer: Miss Irene Robertson Person interviewed: Callie Halsey Williamson, Biscoe, Arkansas Age: 60?

65. Interviewer: Miss Irene Robertson Person interviewed: Charlotte Willis, Madison, Arkansas Age: 63

66. Interviewer: Samuel S. Taylor Person interviewed: Ella Wilson 1611 McGowan Street, Little Rock, Arkansas Age: Claims 100

67. Interviewer: Mrs. Bernice Bowden Person interviewed: Robert Wilson 811 West Pullen Street, Pine Bluff, Arkansas Age: 101

68. Interviewer: Mrs. Bernice Bowden Person interviewed: Tom Windham, 723 Missouri, Pine Bluff, Arkansas Age: 98

69. FOLKLORE SUBJECTS Interviewer: Bernice Bowden Subject: Apparitions Information by: Tom Windham Place of Residence: 723 Missouri St. Pine Bluff, Ark. Occupation: None (Age 92)

70. Pine Bluff District FOLKLORE SUBJECTS Interviewer: Martin - Barker Subject: Ex-Slave Story. Information by: Tom Windham Place of Residence: 1221 Georgia St. Age: 87

71. Interviewer: Mrs. Bernice Bowden Person interviewed: Alice Wise 1112 Indiana Street, Pine Bluff, Arkansas Age: 79

72. Interviewer: Samuel S. Taylor Person interviewed: Frank Wise, 1006 Victory Street, Little Rock, Arkansas Age: 81 to 85

73. Interviewer: Miss Irene Robertson Person interviewed: Lucy Withers, Brinkley, Arkansas Age: 86

74. Interviewer: Mary D. Hudgins Person interviewed: Anna Woods, 426 Grand Avenue

75. Interviewer: Miss Irene Robertson Person interviewed: Cal Woods; R.F.D., Biscoe, Arkansas Age: 85?

76. Interviewer: Miss Irene Robertson Person interviewed: Maggie Woods Brassfield, Ark. Deaner Farm. Age: 70

77. Interviewer: Mrs. Bernice Bowden Person interviewed: Sam Word, 1122 Missouri Street, Pine Bluff, Arkansas Age: 79

78. Interviewer: Mrs. Bernice Bowden Person interviewed: Sam Word 1122 Missouri, Pine Bluff, Arkansas Age: 78

79. Interviewer: Mrs. Bernice Bowden Person interviewed: Ike Worthy 2413 W. 11th Avenue, Pine Bluff, Arkansas Age: 74

80. Interviewer: Samuel S. Taylor Person interviewed: Alice Wright 2418 Center Street, Little Rock, Arkansas Age: About 74

81. Interviewer: Mrs. Bernice Bowden Person interviewed: Hannah Brooks Wright W. 17th, Highland Addition, Pine Bluff, Arkansas Age: 85 Occupation: Laundress

82. Interviewer: Miss Irene Robertson Person interviewed: Tom Yates, Marianna. Arkansas Age: 66

83. Interviewer: Mrs. Bernice Bowden Person interviewed: Annie Young, 913 West Scull Street, Pine Bluff, Arkansas Age: 76

84. Interviewer: Mrs. Bernice Bowden Person interviewed: John Young 925 E. 15th Ave., Pine Bluff, Ark. Age: 92

85. Interviewer: Mrs. Bernice Bowden Person interviewed: John Young 923 E. Fifteenth, Pine Bluff, Arkansas Age: 89

[TR: ***] = Transcriber Note

[HW: ***] = Handwritten Note

# ARKANSAS SLAVE NARRATIVES

## VOLUME II PART 7

*A Folk History of Slavery in the United States
From Interviews with Former Slaves*

## *VOLUME II PART 7*

**TYPEWRITTEN RECORDS PREPARED BY
THE FEDERAL WRITERS' PROJECT
1936-1938
ASSEMBLED BY
THE LIBRARY OF CONGRESS PROJECT
WORK PROJECTS ADMINISTRATION
FOR THE DISTRICT OF COLUMBIA
SPONSORED BY THE LIBRARY OF CONGRESS**

WASHINGTON 1941

**Interviews Prepared by
the Federal Writers' Project of
the Works Progress Administration
for the State of Arkansas**

# ARKANSAS SLAVE NARRATIVES

[TR: ***] = Transcriber Note

[HW: ***] = Handwritten Note

**Interviewer: Irene Robertson**
**Subject: NEGRO LORE**
**Story:—Information**

**This information given by: Charlie Vaden**
**Place of Residence: Hazen, Green Grove, Ark.**
**Occupation: Farming**
**Age:** 77

[TR: Information moved from bottom of first page.]

Charlie Vaden's father ran away and went to the war to fight. He was a slave and left his owner. His mother died when he was five years old but before she died she gave Charlie to Mrs. Frances Owens (white lady). She came to Des Arc and ran the City Hotel. He never saw his father till he was grown. He worked for Mrs. Owens. He never did run with colored folks then. He nursed her grandchildren, Guy and Ira Brown. When he was grown he bought a farm at Green Grove. It consisted of a house and forty-seven acres of land. He farmed two years. A fortune teller came along and told him he was going to marry but he better be careful that they wouldn't live together or he might "drop out." He went ahead and married like he was "fixing" to do. They just couldn't get along, so they got divorced.

They had the wedding at her house and preacher Isarel Thomas (colored) married them and they went on to his house. He don't remember how she was dressed except in white and he had a "new outfit too."

Next he married Lorine Rogers at the Green Grove Church and took her home. She fell off the porch with a tub of clothes and died from it just about a year after they married.

He married again at the church and lived with her twenty years. They had four girls and four boys. She died from the change of life.

The last wife he didn't live with either. She is still living.

Had another fortune teller tell his fortune. She said, "Uncle, you are pretty good but be careful or you'll be walking around begging for victuals." He said it had nearly come to that now except it hurt him to walk. (He can hardly walk.) He believes some of what the fortune tellers tell comes true. He has been on the same farm since 1887, which is forty-nine years, and did fine till four years ago. He can't work, couldn't pay taxes, and has lost his land.

He was paralyzed five months, helpless as a baby, couldn't dress himself. An herb doctor settled at Green Grove and used herbs for tea and poultices and cured him. The doctors and the law run him out of there. His name was Hopkins from Popular Bluff, Missouri.

Charlie Vaden used to have rheumatism and he carried a buckeye in each pants pocket to make the rheumatism lighter. He thought it did some good.

He has a birthmark. Said his mother must have craved pig tails. He never had enough pig tails to eat in his life. The butchers give them to him when he comes to Hazen or Des Arc. He said he would "fight a circle saw for a pig tail."

He can't remember any old songs or old tales. In fact he was too small when his mother died (five years old).

He believes in herb medicine of all kinds but can't remember except garlic poultice is good for neuralgia. Sassafras is a good tea, a good blood purifier in the spring of the year.

He knows a weather sign that seldom or never falls. "Thunder in the morning, rain before noon." "Seldom rains at night in July in Arkansas."

He has seen lots of lucky things but doesn't remember them. "It's bad luck to carry hoes and rakes in the living house." "It's bad luck to spy the new moon through bushes or trees."

He doesn't believe in witches, but he believes in spirits that direct your course as long as you are good and do right. He goes to church all the time if they have preaching. Green Grove is a Baptist church. He is not afraid of dead people. "They can't hurt you if they are dead."

---

**Interviewer: Miss Irene Robertson**
**Person interviewed: Ellen Vaden**
**DeValls Bluff, Ark.**
**Age: 83**

" I am 83 years old. My mother come from Georgia. She left all her kin. Our owner was Dave and Luiza Johnson. They had two girls and a boy--Meely, Colly and Tobe. My mother's aunt come to Memphis in slavery time and come to see us. She cooked and bought herself free. The folks what owned her hired her out till they got paid her worth. She died in Memphis. I never heard father say where he come from or who owned him. He lived close by somewhere.

"I don't remember freedom. I know the Ku Klux was bad around Augusta, Arkansas. One time when I was little a crowd of Ku Klux come at about dusk. They told Dave Johnson they wanted water. He told them there was a well full but not bother that woman and her children in the kitchen. Dave Johnson was a Ku Klux himself. They went on down the road and met a colored woman. She knowed their horses. She called some of them by name and they let her alone.

"One time a colored man was settin' by the fire. His wife was sick in bed. He seen the Ku Klux coming and said 'Lord God, here comes the devil.' He run off. They didn't bother her. She told them she was sick. When she got up and well she wouldn't live with that husband no more.

"Up at Bowens Ridge they took some colored men out one night and if they said they was Republicans they let them go but if they said they was Democrats they whooped them so hard they nearly killed some of them. Some said they was bushwhackers or carpet baggers and not Ku Klux.

"I am a country-raised woman. I had a light stroke and cain't work in the field. I get $8.00 and commodities. I like to live here very well. I don't meddle with young folks business. Seems like they do mighty foolish things to me. Times been changing ever since I come in this world. It is the people cause the times to change. I wouldn't know how to start to vote."

---

**Interviewer: Miss Irene Robertson**
**Person interviewed: Nettie Van Buren, Clarendon, Arkansas**
**Ex school-teacher**
**Age: 62**

"My mother was named Isabel Porter Smith. She come from Springville. Rev. Porter brought her to Mississippi close to Holly Springs. Then she come to Batesville, Arkansas. He owned her. He was a circuit rider. I think he was a Presbyterian minister. I heard her say they brought her to Arkansas when she was a small girl. She nursed and cooked all the time. After freedom she went with Reverend Porter's relatives to work for them. I know so very little about what she said about slavery.

"My father was raised in North Carolina. His name was Jerry Smith and his master he called Judge Smith. My father made all he ever had farmin'. He knew how to raise cotton. He owned a home. This is his home (a nice home on River Street in Clarendon) and 80 acres. He sold this farm two miles from here after he had paralysis, to live on.

"My parents had two girls and two boys. They all dead but me. My mother's favorite song was "Oh How I Love Jesus Because He First Loved Me." They

23

come here because my mother had a brother down here and she heard it was such fine farmin' land.

"When I was a little girl my father was a Presbyterian so he sent me to boardin' school in Cotton Plant and then sent me to Jacksonville, Illinois. I worked my board out up there. Mrs. Dr. Carroll got me a place to work. My sister learned to sew. She sewed for the public till her death. She sewed for both black and white folks. I stretches curtains now if I can get any to stretch and I irons. It give me rheumatism to wash. I used to wash and iron.

"My husband cooks on a Government derrick boat. He gets $1.25 and his board. They have the very best things to eat. He likes the work if he can stay well. He can cook pies and fancy cookin'. They like that. Say they can't hardly get somebody work long because they want to be in town every night.

"We have one child. I used to be a primary teacher here at Clarendon.

"I never have voted. My husband votes but I don't know what he thinks about it.

"I try to look at the present conditions in an encouraging way. The young people are so extravagant. The old folks in need. The thing most discouraging is the strangers come in and get jobs home folks could do and need and they can't get jobs and got no money to leave on nor no place to go. People that able to work don't work hard as they ought and people could and willin' to work can't get jobs. Some of the young folks do sure live wild lives. They think only of the present times. A few young folks are buying homes but not half of them got a home. They work where they let 'em have a room or a house. Different folks live all kinds of ways."

---

**Name of Interviewer: Samuel S. Taylor**
**Person Interviewed: Adelaide J. Vaughn**
**1122 Cross Street, Little Rock, Arkansas**
**Age: 69**

"I was born in Huntsville, Alabama. My mother brought me from there when I was five years old. She said she would come to Arkansas because she had heard so much talk about it. But when she struck the Arkansas line, she didn't like it and she wanted to go back. I have heard her say why but I don't remember now; I done forgot. She thought she wouldn't like it here, but she did after she stayed a while.

"My bronchial tubes git all stopped up and make it hard for me to talk. Phlegm gits all around. I been bothered with them a good while now.

"My mother, she was sold from her father when she was four years old. The rest of the children were grown then. Master Hickman was the one who bought her. I don't know the one that sold her. Hickman had a lot of children her age and he raised her up with them. They were nice to her all the time.

"Once the pateroles came near capturing her. But she made it home and they didn't catch her.

"Mr. Candle hired her from her master when she was about eighteen years old. He was nice to her but his wife was mean. Just because mother wouldn't do everything the other servants said Mis' Candle wanted to whip her. Mother said she knew that Mis' Candle couldn't whip her alone. But she was 'fraid that she would have Sallie, another old Negro woman slave, and Kitty, a young Negro woman slave, to help whip her.

"One day when it was freezing cold, she wanted mother to stand out in the hall with Sallie and Clara and wash the glasses in boiling hot water. She was making her do that because she thought she was uppity and she wanted to punish her. When mother went out, she rattled the dishes 'round in the pan and broke them. They was all glasses. Mis' Candle heard them breaking and come out to see

25

about it. She wanted to whip mother but she was 'fraid to do it while she was alone; so she waited till her husband come home. When he come she told him. He said she oughtn't to have sent them out in the cold to wash the glasses because nobody could wash dishes outside in that cold weather.

"The first morning she was at Mis' Candle's, they called her to eat and they didn't have nothing but black molasses and corn bread for mother's meal. The other two ate it but mother didn't. She asked for something else. She said she wasn't used to eating that--that she ate what her master and mistress ate at home.

"Mis' Candle didn't like that to begin with. She told my mother that she was a smart nigger. She told mother to do one thing and then before she could do it, she would tell her do something else. Mother would just go on doing the first thing till she finished that, and Mis' Candle would git mad. But it wasn't nobody's fault but her own.

"She asked mother to go out and git water from the spring on a rainy day. Mother wouldn't go. Finally mother got tired and went back home. Her mistress heard what she had to tell her about the place she'd been working. Then she said mother did right to quit. She had worked there for three or four months. They meant to keep her but she wouldn't stay. Mis' Hickman went over and collected her money.

"When mother worked out, the people that hired her paid her owners. Her owners furnished her everything she wanted to eat and clothes to wear, and all the money she earned went to them.

"Mis' Candle begged Mr. Hickman to let him have mother back. He said he'd talk to his wife and she wouldn't mistreat her any more but mama said that she didn't want to go back and Mrs. Hickman said, 'No, she doesn't want to go back and I wouldn't make her.' And the girls said, 'No, mama, don't let her go back.' And Mis' Hickman said, 'No, she was raised with my girls and I am not going to let her go back.'

"The Hickmans had my mother ever since she was four years old. My grandfather was allowed to go a certain distance with her when she was sold away from him. He walked and carried her in his arms. Mama said that when he had gone as far as they would let him go, he put her in the wagon and turned his head away. She said she wondered why he didn't look at her; but later she understood that he hated so bad to 'part from her and couldn't do nothing to prevent it that he couldn't bear to look at her.

"Since I have been grown I have worked with some people at Newport. I stayed with them there and married there, and had all my children there.

"I heard the woman I lived with, a woman named Diana Wagner, tell how her mistress said, 'Come on, Diana, I want you to go with me down the road a piece.' And she went with her and they got to a place where there was a whole lot of people. They were putting them up on a block and selling them just like cattle. She had a little nursing baby at home and she broke away from her mistress and them and said, 'I can't go off and leave my baby.' And they had to git some men and throw her down and hold her to keep her from goin' back to the house. They sold her away from her baby boy. They didn't let her go back to see him again. But she heard from him after he became a young man. Some one of her friends that knowed her and knowed she was sold away from her baby met up with this boy and got to questioning him about his mother. The white folks had told him his mother's name and all. He told them and they said, 'Boy, I know your mother. She's down in Newport.' And he said, 'Gimme her address and I'll write to her and see if I can hear from her.' And he wrote. And the white people said they heard such a hollering and shouting goin' on they said, 'What's the matter with Diana?' And they came over to see what was happening. And she said, 'I got a letter from my boy that was sold from me when he was a nursing baby.' She had me write a letter to him. I did all her writing for her and he came to see her. I didn't get to see him. I was away when he come. She said she was willing to die that the Lord let her live to see her baby again and had taken care of him through all these years.

"My father's name was Peter Warren and my mother was named Adelaide Warren. Before she was married she went by her owner's name, Hickman. My daddy belonged to the Phillips but he didn't go in their name. He went in the Warren's name. He did that because he liked them. Phillips was his real father, but he sold him to the Warrens and he took their name and kept it. They treated him nice and he just stayed on in their name. He didn't marry till after both of them were free. He met her somewheres away from the Hickman's. They married in Alabama.

"Mama was born and mostly reared in Virginia and then come to Alabama. That's where I was born, in Alabama. And they left there and came here. I was four years old when they come here.

"I never did hear what my father did in slavery time. He was a twin. The most he took notice of he said was his brother and him settin' on an old three-legged stool. And his mother had left some soft soap on the fire. His brother saw that the pot was goin' to turn over and he jumped up. My father tried to get up too but the stool turned over and caught him, caught his little dress and held him and the hot soap ran over his dress and on to his bare skin. It left a big burn on his side long as he lived. His mother was there close to the house because she knowed the soap was on and those two little boys were in there. She heard him crying and ran in and carried him to her master. He got the doctor and saved him. My father's mother didn't do nothing after that but 'tend to that baby. Her master loved those little boys and kept her and didn't sell her because of them. (The underscoring is the interviewer's--ed.) That was his last master--Warren. Warren loved him more than his real father did. Warren said he knew my father would never live after he had such a burn. But he did live. They never did let him do much work after the accident.

"I think my father's master, Warren--I can't remember his first name--farmed for a living.

"My father and mother had five children. I don't know how many brothers my father had. I have heard my mother say she had four sisters. I never heard her say nothin' 'bout no brothers--just sisters.

"I had six children. Got three living and three dead. They was grown though when they died. I had three boys and three girls. I got two boys living and one girl. The boy in St. Louis does pretty well. But the other in Little Rock doesn't have much luck. If he'd get out of Little Rock, he would find more to do. The one in St. Louis don't make much now because they done cut wages. He's a dining-car waiter. This girl what's here, she does all she can for me. She has a husband and my husband is dead. He's been dead a long time.

"I belong to Bethel A.M.E. Church. You know where that is. Rev. Campbell is a good man. We had him eight years. Then we got Brother Wilson one year and then they put Campbell back.

"I don't know what to think of these young people. Some of them is running wild.

"When I was working for myself, I was generally a maid. But that is been a long time ago. I washed and ironed and done laundry work when I was able a long time ago. But I can't do it now. I can't do it for myself now. I washed for myself a little and I got the flu and got in bad health. That was about four years ago. I reckon it was the flu; I never did have no doctor. When I take the least little cold, it comes back on me."

### Interviewer's Comment

This old lady appears nearer eighty than sixty-nine, and she speaks with the sureness of an eyewitness.

---

## Interviewer: Mrs. Blanche Edwards
## Person interviewed: Emmeline Waddille (deceased)
## Lonoke County, Arkansas
## Age: 106

She immigrated with her owner, L.W.C. Waddille, to Lonoke County in 1851, coming to Hickory Plains and then to Brownsville. They moved from Hayburn, Georgia in a covered wagon drawn by oxen.

She lived with a great-granddaughter, Mrs. John High, seven miles north of Lonoke, until 1932, when she died. She had nursed six generations of the

Waddille family. She was born a deaf-mute but her hearing and speech were restored many years ago when lightening struck a tree under which she was standing.

Emmeline told of how they would stop for the night on the rough journey, and while the men fed the stock, the women and slaves would cook the evening meal of hoecake, fried venison, and coffee. The women slept in the wagons and the men would sleep on the creek watching for wild life. With other pioneers, they suffered all the hardships and dangers incident to the settling of the new country more than three-fourths of a century ago.

Emmeline always had good care. She worked hard and faithfully and was amply rewarded.

---

[HW: High]

**STATE—Arkansas**
**NAME OF WORKER—Blanche Edwards**
**ADDRESS—Lonoke, Arkansas**
**DATE—October 20, 1938**
**SUBJECT—An Old Slave**

[TR: Repetitive information deleted from subsequent pages.]

**Circumstances of Interview**

1. Name and address of informant—Mrs. John G. High **[TR: Emiline Waddell]**, living nine miles north of Lonoke, Arkansas.

2. Date and time of interview—October 20, 1938.

3. Place of interview—At the home of Mrs. John G. High, nine miles north of Lonoke.

4. Name and address of person, if any, who put you in touch with informant—

5. Name and address of person, if any, accompanying you—

6. Description of room, house, surroundings, etc.

**Text of Interview**

Emiline Waddell, a former slave of the L.W. Waddell family, lived to be 106 years old, and was active up to her death.

She was born a slave in 1826 at Haben county, Georgia, a slave of Claybourne Waddell, who emigrated to Brownsville, in 1851, in covered wagons, oxen drawn.

Her "white folks" were three weeks making the trip from the ferry across the Mississippi to old Brownsville; after traveling all day through the bad and boggy woods, at the end of their rough journey at eventide, the movers dismounted and began hasty preparations for the night. While the men were feeding the stock and providing temporary quarters, the women assisted the slaves in preparing the evening meal, of hoe-cake, fried venison and coffee. Then the women and children would sleep in the wagons while the men kept watch for wild life.

Mammy Emiline was a faithful old black mammy, true to life and traditions, and refused her freedom, at the close of the war, as wanted to stay and raise "Old Massa's chilluns," which she did, for she was nursing her sixth generation in the Waddell family at the time of her death. Even to that generation there was a close tie between the southern child and his or her black mammy. A strange almost unbelievable thing happened to Emiline; she was born a deaf mute, but her hearing and speech was restored many years before her death, when lightening struck a tree under which she was standing.

Superstitious beliefs were strong in her and her tales of "hants" were to "her little white chilluns", really true but hair-raising. Then she would talk and live again the "days that are no more", telling them of the happy prosperous, sunny land, in her negro dialect, and then tell of the ruin and desolation behind the Yankees; the hard times my white folks had in the reconstruction days—negro and carpetbag rule; then give them glimpses of good—much courage, some heart and human feeling; perhaps ending with an outburst of the negro spiritual, her favorite being, "Swing low, sweet chariot, coming for to carry me home."

After a faithful service of 106 years, Emiline died in 1932 at the home of Mrs. John G. High, a great-granddaughter of L.W.C. Waddell living nine miles north of Lonoke, and the grown up great-great-grandchildren still miss Mammy.

---

**Interviewer: Samuel S. Taylor**
**Person interviewed: Henry Waldon**
**816 Walnut Street. North Little Rock, Arkansas**
**Age: 84**

"I was plowing when they surrendered. I had just learned to plow, and was putting up some land. My young master come home and was telling me the War was ended and we was all free.

"I was born in Lauderdale County, Mississippi. I think it was about 1854. My father's name [HW: was] ----, my mother's [HW: was] ----, I knew them both.

"My mother belonged to Sterling and my father belonged to a man named Huff—Richmond Huff.

"We lived in Lauderdale County. Huff wouldn't sell my father and my people wouldn't sell my mother. They lived about a mile or so apart. They didn't marry in them days. The niggers didn't, that is. Father would just come every Saturday night to see my mother. His cabin was about three miles from her's. We moved from Lauderdale County to Scott County, Mississippi, and that separated mama and papa. They never did meet again. Of course, I mean it was the white people that moved, but they carried mama and us with them. Papa and mama never did meet again before freedom, and they didn't meet afterwards.

"My mother had twelve children—eight girls and four boys. She had one by a man named Peter Smith. She was away from her husband then. She had four by my father—two boys and two girls; my father's name was Peter Huff. My mother's name was Mary Sterling. I never did see my father no more after we moved away from him.

"My father made cotton and corn, plowed and hoed in slavery time. His old master had seventy-five or eighty hands. His old master treated him pretty rough. He whipped them about working. He never hired no overseer over them. When he whipped them he took their shirts off and whipped them on their naked backs. He cut the blood out of some of them. He never did rub no salt nor vinegar in their wounds. His youngest son done his overseeing. He would whip them sometime but he wasn't tight on them like some that I knowed.

"A fellow by the name of Jim Holbert was mean to his slaves as a man could be. He would whip them night and day. Work them till dark; then they would eat supper. Cook their own supper. Had nothing to cook but a little meat and bread and molasses. Then they would go back and bale up three or four bales of cotton. Some nights they work till twelve o'clock then get up before daylight—'round four o'clock—and cook their breakfast and go to work again. That was on Jim Holbert and Lard Moore's place. Them was two different men and two different places—plantations. They whipped their slaves a good deal—always beating down on somebody. They made their backs sore. Their backs would be bleeding just like they cut it with knives. Then they would wash it down with water and salt.

"On my master's farm, each one cooked in his own cabin. While the hands were working, my master left one child, the largest, stay there and taken care of the little ones.

"They had bloodhounds too; they'd run you away in the woods. Send for a man that had hounds to track you if you run away. They'd run you and bay you, and a

33

white man would ride up there and say, 'If you hit one of them hounds, I'll blow your brains out.' He'd say 'your damn brains.' Them hounds would worry you and bite you and have you bloody as a beef, but you dassent to hit one of them. They would tell you to stand still and put your hands over your privates. I don't guess they'd have killed you but you believed they would. They wouldn't try to keep the hounds off of you; they would set them on you to see them bite you. Five or six or seven hounds bitin' you on every side and a man settin' on a horse holding a doubled shotgun on you.

"My old miss's sister hired slave women out to old Jim Holbert once. One of them was in a delicate state, and they dug a hole and put her stomach down in it and whipped her till she could hardly walk.

"Holbert lived to see the niggers freed. All of his slaves left him pretty well when freedom come. He managed to hold on to his money. He didn't go to the War. He was pretty old. He had two sons in the War—his wife had one in there and he had one. One of them got wounded but he didn't die.

"My mistress's oldest son, Ed Sterling, got shot in the Civil War. He got shot right in the side at Franklin, Tennessee. It tore his whole side off—near about killed him. But he lived to ride paterole. He was mean. Catch a man in bed with his wife at night, he'd whip him and make him go home. He was the meanest man in the world. All the other sons were better than he was. His name was Ed Sterling.

"The first thing I remember was work. You weren't allowed to remember nothing but work in slave times and you got whipped about that. You weren't allowed to go nowhere but carry the mules out to the pasture to eat grass. Sometimes they jump the fence and go over in the field and eat corn. Me and another fellow named Sandy used to watch them all day Sunday. Watching the mules and working in the fields through the week was the first work I remember. Me and my sister worked on one row. The two of us made a hand. She is down in Texas somewheres now. They taken her from old lady Sterling's place. She give them to her son and he carried them down in Texas. He had a broken leg and never did go to the war. If he did, I never knowed nothing about it.

"None of the masters never give me anything. None of them as I knows of never give anything to any of the slaves when they freed 'em. Never give a devilish thing. Told them that they was free as they was and that they could stay there and help them make crops if they wanted to. The biggest part of them stayed. The rest went away. Their husbands taken them away.

"Right after the war my mother married an old fellow who used to be old Holbert's nigger driver. He stayed on Sterling's place one night. He stayed there a year. Then he married my mother and went to old Holbert's place and of course, we had to go too. I stayed there and worked for him. And my mama too and the two youngest sisters and the youngest brother stayed with me. I run away from him in '86. I went down the railroad about five miles and an old colored fellow give me a job. He used to belong to the railroad boss.

"I worked nearly two years on that railroad; then I left and come on down to Arkansas. I have been right here on this spot about forty years. I don't know how long it is been since I first come here, but it is been a long time ago. I paid fire insurance on this place for thirty-nine years. I lived over the river before I came to North Little Rock. I worked for the railroad company thirty-eight years. It's been fifteen years since I was able to work—maybe longer.

"I belong to Little Bethel Church (A.M.E.) here in North Little Rock. I been a member of that church more than thirty-five years.

"I have been married twice, and I am the father of three children that are living and two that dead—Tommy, Jim, Ewing, Mayzetta, and the baby. He was too young to have a name when he died.

"I think things is worse than they ever was. Everything we get we have to pay for, and then pay for paying for it. If it wasn't for my wife I could hardly live because I don't get much from the railroad company."

---

**Interviewer: Mary D. Hudgins**
**Person interviewed: Aunt Clara Walker     Aged: 111**
**Home: "Flatwoods" district, Garland County. Own property.**

## Story by Aunt Clara Walker

"You'll have to wait a minute ma'am. Dis cornbread can't go down too fas'. Yes ma'am, I likes cornbread. I eats it every meal. I wouldn't trade just a little cornbread for all de flour dat is.

Where-bouts was I born? I was born right here in Arkansas. Dat is it was between an on de borders of it an dat state to de south—yes ma'am, dat's right, Louisiana. My mother was a slave before me. She come over from de old country, she was a-runnin' along one day front of a—a—dat stripedy animal—a tiger? an' a man come along on an elephant and scoop her up an' put her on a ship.

Yes ma'am. My name's Clara Walker. I was born Clara Jones, cause my pappy's name was Jones. But lots of folks called me Clara Cornelius, cause Mr. Cornelius was de man what owned me. Did you ever hear of a child born wid a veil over its face? Well I was one of dem! What it mean? Why it means dat you can see spirits an' ha'nts, an all de other creatures nobody else can see.

Yes ma'am, some children is born dat way. You see dat great grandchild of mine lyin' on de floor? He's dat way. He kin see 'em too. Is many of 'em around here? Lawsey dey's as thick as piss-ants. What does dey look like? Some of 'em looks like folks; an' some of 'em looks like hounds. When dey sees you, dey says "Howdy!" an' if you don't speak to 'em dey takes you by your shoulders an dey shakes you. Maybe dey hits you on de back. An' if you go over to de bed an lies in de bed an' goes to sleep, dey pulls de cover off you. You got to be polite to 'em. What makes 'em walk around? Well, I got it figgured out dis way. Dey's dissatisfied. Dey didn't have time to git dey work done while dey was alive.

Dat greatgrandchild of mine, he kin see 'em too. Now my eight grandchildren an' my three children what's alivin' none of 'em can see de spirits. Guess dat greatgrandchild struck way back. I goes way back. My ol' master what had to go to de war, little 'fore it was over told me when he left dat I was 39 years old. Somebody figgured it out for me dat I's 111 now. Dat makes me pretty old, don't it?

36

There was another fellow on a joinin' plantation. He was a witch doctor. Brought him over from Africa. He didn't like his master, 'cause he was mean. So he make a little man out of mud. An' he stick thorns in its back. Sure 'nuff, his master got down with a misery in his back. An' de witch doctor let de thorn stay in de mud-man until he thought his master had got 'nuff punishment. When he tuck it out, his master got better.

Did I got to school. No ma'am. Not to book school. Dey wouldn't let culled folks git no learnin'. When I was a little girl we skip rope an' play high-spy (I Spy). All we had to do was to sweep de yard an go after de cows an' de pigs an de sheep. An' dat was fun, cause dey was lots of us children an we all did it together.

When I was 13 years old my ol' mistress put me wid a doctor who learned me how to be a midwife. Dat was cause so many women on de plantation was catchin' babies. I stayed wid dat doctor, Dr. McGill his name was, for 5 years. I got to be good. Got so he'd sit down an' I'd do all de work.

When I come home, I made a lot o' money for old miss. Lots of times, didn't sleep regular or git my meals on time for three—four days. Cause when dey call, I always went. Brought as many white as culled children. I's brought most 200, white an' black since I's been in Hot Springs. Brought a little white baby—to de Wards it was—dey lived jest down de lane—brought dat baby 'bout 7 year ago.

I's brought lots of 'em an' I ain't never lost a case. You know why. It's cause I used my haid. When I'd go in, I'd take a look at de woman, an' if it was beyond me, I'd say, 'Dis is a doctor case. Dis ain't no case for a midwife. You git a doctor.' An' dey'd have to get one. I'd jes' stan' before de lookin' glass, an' I wouldn't budge. Dey couldn't make me.

I made a lot of money for ol' miss. But she was good to me. She give me lots of good clothes. Those clothes an my mother's clothes burned up in de fire I had a few years ago right on dis farm. Lawsey I hated loosin' dose clothes I had when I was a girl more dan anything I lost. An' I didn't have to work in de fields. In between times I cooked an' I would jump in de loom. Yes, ma'am I could weave good. Did my yards every day. I weave cloth for dresses—fine dresses you would use thread as thin as dat you sews wid today—I weaves cloth for underclothes, an fo handkerchiefs an for towels. Den I weaves nits and lice.

What's dat—well you see it was kind corse cloth de used for clothes like overalls. It mas sort of speckeldy all over—dat's why dey called it nits and lice.

Law, I used to be good once, but after I got all burned up I wasn't good for so much. It happened dis way. A salt lick was on a nearby plantation. Ever body who wanted salt, dey had to send a hand to help make it. I went over one day—an workin' around I stepped on a live coal. I move quick an' I fall plum over into a salt vat. Before dey got me out I was pretty near ruined.

What did dey do? Dey killed a hog—fresh killed a hog. An' dey fry up de fat—fry it up wid some of de hog hairs an' dey greesed me good. An' it took all de fire out of de burns. Dey kept me greezed for a long time. I was sick nearly six months. Dey was good to me.

An one day, young miss, she married. Ol' miss give me to her 'long of 23 others. Twenty four was all she could spare an' keep some for herself an save enough for de other children. We went to California. Young Miss was good, but her husband was mean. He give me de only white folks whippin I ever had. Ol' miss never had to whip her slaves. I was tryin' to cook on an earth stove—dat's why it happen. Did you ever hear of an earth stove? Well, dey make sort of drawers out of dirt. You burn wood in 'em. After you git used to it you kin cook on it good. But dat day I was busy an' I burned de biscuits. An' he whip me.

I run off. I knew in general de way home. When I come to de Brazos river it looked most a mile across. But I jump in an' I swim it. One day I done found a pearl handled pocket knife. A few days later I meet up wid a white boy. An' he say its his knife, an' I say, 'White boy, I know dat ain't your knife, an' you know it ain't. But if you'll write me out a free pass, I'll give it to you.' An' so he wrote it. After dat, I could walk right up to de front gates an ask for somthin' to eat. Cause I had a paper sayin' I was Clara Jones an' I was goin' home to my ol' mistress Mis' Cornelius. Please paterollers to leave me alone. An' folks along de way, dey'd take me in an' feed me. Dey'd give me a place to stay an fix me up a lunch to take along. Dey'd say, "Clara, you's a good nigger. You's a goin' home to your ol' miss, so we's goin' to do for you."

An' I got within five miles of home before dey catch me. An' my ol' miss won't let me go back. She keep me an' send another one in my place. An' de war kept on, an ol' massa had to go. An' word come dat he been killed.

Yes, 'em, some folks run off, an' some of 'em stayed. Finally ol' miss refugeed a lot of us to California. What is it to refugee. Well, you see, suppose you was afraid dat somebody go in' to take your property an' you run 'em away off somewhere—how you come to know.

When de war was over, young miss she come in an she say, 'Clara, you's as free as I am.' 'No, I ain't.' says I. 'Yes, you is,' says she. 'What you goin' to do?' 'I's goin' to stay an' work for you.' says I. 'No' says she, 'you ain't cause I can't pay you.' 'Well,' says I, 'I'll go home to see my old mother.' 'Tell you what,' says she, 'I ain't got nuff money to send you, only part—so you go down to whar' dey is a'pannin' gold. You kin git a Job at $2.00 per day.'

Many's a day I've stood in water up to my waist pannin' gold. In dem days dey worked women jest like men. I worked hard, an' young miss took care of me. When I got ready to come home I bought my stage fare an' I carried $300 on me back to my ol' mother.

De trip took six weeks. Everywhere de stage would stop young miss had writ a note to somebody and de stage coach men give it to 'em an dey took care of me—good care.

When I got home to my mother I found dat ol' miss had give all of 'em somthin' along with settin 'em free. My mother had 12 children so she git de mos'. She git a horse, a milk cow, 8 killin' hogs and 50 bushels of corn. She moved off to a little house on ol' miss's plantation and make a crop on halvers. She stay on dar for three—four years. Den she move off into another county where she could go to meetin without havin' to cross de river. An' I stayed on wid her an help her farm—I could plow as good as a man in dem days.

Finally I hear dat you could make more money in Hot Springs, so I come to see. My mother was dead by dat time. De first year I made a crop for Mr. Clay—my granddaughter cooks and tends to children for some of his folks today. When I went to town an I washed at de Arlington hotel. It wasn't de fine place it is today.

It was jest boards like dis cabin of mine. An I washed at another hotel—what was it—down across de creek from de Arlington. Yes ma'am, dat's it. De Grand Central—it was grand too—for dem days. An' I cooked for Dr. McMasters. An' I cooked for Colonel Rector—de Rectors had lots of money in dem days. I could make a weddin' cake good as anybody—with, a 'gagement ring in it. I could make it fine—tho I don't know but two letters in de book an' thoses is A and B.

I married Mr. Walker. He was a hod carrier when dey built de old red brick Arlington. I remember lots of things dat happened here. I remember seein' de smoke from de fire—dat big one. We was a livin' near Picket Springs—you don't know whare dat is. Well, does you know where de soldier's breast work was—now I git you on to remembering.

Den, later on we moved out an' got a farm near Hawes. I traded dat place for dis one. Yes, ma'am I likes livin' in de country. Never did like livin' in town.

I don't right know whether culled folks wanted to be free or not. Lots of 'em didn't rightly understand, Ol' miss was good to hers. Some of 'em wasn't. She give 'em things before an she give 'em things after. Of course, we went back an' we washed for 'em. But one mortal blessin. Ol' miss had made her girls learn how to cook an' wait on themselves.

Now take de Combinders. Dey was on de next plantation. Dey was mean. Many a time you could hear de bull whip, clear over to our place, PLOP, PLOP. An' if dey died, dey jest wrapped 'em in cloth an' dig a trench, an' plow right over 'em. An' when de war was over, dey wouldn't turn dey slaves loose. An de Federals marched in an' marched 'em off. An' ol' Mis' Combinder she holler out an she say, 'What my girls goin' to do? Dey ain't never dressed deyselves in dey life. We can't cook? What we do?' An' de soldiers didn't pay no attention. Dey just marched 'em off.

An' ol' man Combinder he lay down an' he have a chill an' he die. He die because day take his property away from him.

Yes, ma'am, Thank you for the quarter. I's goin' to buy snuff. I gets along good. My grandson he hauls wood for de paper mill. An' my granddaughters dey works for folks cooks an takes care of children. I had a good crop dis year. I'll have meat, I got lots of corn, an' I got other crops. We're gettin' along nice, mighty nice. Thank you ma'am."

---

**Interviewer: Miss Irene Robertson**
**Person interviewed: Henry Walker, Hazen, Arkansas**
**Age: 80**

I was born nine miles south of Nashville, Tennessee. The first I ever knowed or heard of a war, I saw a lot of the funniest wagons coming up to the house from the road. I called the old mistress. She looked out the window and pushed me back up in the corner and shot the door. She was so scared. I thought them things they had on their coats (buttons) was pretty. I found out they was brass buttons. I peeped out a crack it was already closed 'cept a big crack, I seed through. Well, the wagons was high in front and high in the back and sunk in the middle. Had pens in the wheels instead of axels. Wagon had a box instead of a bed. The wagons would hold a crib full of corn. They loaded up everything on the place there was to eat and carried it off. My folks and the other folks was in the field. Colored folks didn't like 'em taking all they had to eat and had stored up to live on. They didn't leave a hog nor a chicken, nor anything else they could find. They drove off all the cows and calves they could find. Colonel Sam Williams, the old master, soon did go to war then. The folks had a hard time making a living. Old mistress had four girls and her baby Ed was one day older than I was. The children of the hands played around in the woods and every place and stayed in the field if they was big enough to do any work. Old mistress had all the children pick up scaley barks and hickory nuts and chestnuts and walnuts. She put them in barrels. She sold some of them. She had a heap of sugar maple trees. They put an elder funnel to run the sap in buckets. We carried that and she boiled it down to brown sugar. She had up pick up chips to burn when she simmered it down or made soap. She kept all the children hunting ginsing up in the mountains. She kept it in sacks. A man come by and buy it. We hunted chenqupins down in the swamps. There was lots of walnut trees in the woods.

No the slaves didn't leave Colonel Williams. He left them. He brought me and Ed and we went back and moved to the old Williams farm on Arkansas River close to Little Rock. Then he sent for my folks. They come in wagons. They worked for him a long time and scattered about. I stayed at his house till he said "Henry, you are grown; you better look out for yourself now." Ed was gone. He sent all the girls off to school and Ed too. They taught me if I wanted to learn but I didn't care much about it. I went to the colored school and Ed to the white school. He learned pretty well. I never did like to 'sociate or stay 'bout colored folks and I didn't like to mind 'em. Old mistress show did brush me out sometimes and they called my mother to tend to me. When I was real little they drove the hands to the block to be sold out along the road. Old mistress say: "If you don't be good and mind we'll send yare off and sell you wid 'em." That scared me worse than a whooping. Never did see anybody sold. Heard them talk a heap about it. When one of them wouldn't work and lay out in the woods, or they wouldn't mind they soon got sold off. They mated a heap of them and sold them for speculation. No mam I didn't like slavery. We had plenty to eat but they worked for all they got. Had good fires and good warm houses and good clothes but I did not like the way they give out the provisions. They blowed a horn and measured out the weeks paratta for every family. They cooked at the cabins for their own families. There was several springs and a deep rock walled well at old mistress' house. Old mistress always lived in a fine house. I slept at my mother's house nearly all the time. She had a big family. White folks raised me up to play with Ed till I thought I was white. They taught me to do right and I ain't forgot it. I never was arrested. I married three times, bought three marriage license all in Prairie County. All three wives died.

I owns dis house 'cept a mortgage of $50. One of my boys got in a difficulty. I don't know where he is to get him to pay it off. The other boy he's not man enough either to pay it off.

I never did know jess when the Civil War did close. I kept hearing 'em say we are free. I didn't see much difference only when Colonel Williams come back times wasn't so hard. Then he sold out and come to Arkansas. Then each family raised his own hogs and chickens and finally got to have cows.

I was as scared of the Ku Klux Klan as of rattlesnakes. In Tennessee they come up the road and back just after dark. They rode all night and if you wasn't on your master's own land and didn't have a pass from him or the overseer they would set the dogs on you and run you home. Sometimes they would whip them. Take them home to the old master. I never heard of no uprisings. People loved each other better then than now. They didn't have so much idle time. There was always some work to be doing. When they didn't mind they run them with dogs and whipped them. The overseer and paddyrollers seed about that. The first day of the year everybody went up to hear the rules and see who was to be the overseer. Then they knowed what to do for the year. They never did kill nobody. No mam that was too costly. They had work according to their strength and age. The Ku Klux was to keep order.

I been living in Hazen forty or fifty years. All I ever have done was farm sometimes one-half-for-the-other and sometimes on share-crop.

I have voted but not lately. I votes a Republican ticket. I votes that way because it was the Republicans that set us free, I always heard it said. I jess belongs to that party. Seems lack we gets easier times when the Democrats reign. Colonel Williams was a Democrat.

The young folks are not as well off as I was at their age. They are restless and won't work unless they gets big pay and they spends the money too easy. The colored people are too idle and orderless. They fight and hate one another and roam around in too much confusion.

I gets from $3 to $8 last month from the Sociable Welfare. My children helps me mighty little. They got their own children to see after and don't make much.

Colonel Williams and Ed are both dead. They did give me a lot of fine clothes when I went to see them as long as they lived. I don't know where the girls hab gone. Scattered around. I oughter never left my good old home and white folks. They was show always mighty good to me.

I never could sing much. I used to give the Rebbel Yell. Colonel Yopp give me a dime every time I give it. Since he died I ain't yelled it no more. I learned it from Colonel Williams. I jess took it up hearing him about the place.

Interviewer: Irene Robertson
Subject: Ex-Slave-Hunting
Story:—Information

This information given by: Henry Walker
Place of Residence: Hazen, Arkansas
Occupation: Farmer.
Age: 78

[TR: Information moved from bottom of first page.]

Henry Walker was born nine miles south of Nashville, Tennessee. Remembered the soldiers and ran to the windows to see them pass. One day he saw a lot of soldiers coming to the house. Henry ran in ahead and said out loud, "them Yankeys are coming up here." The mistress slapped Henry, hid him and slammed the doors. The soldiers did not get in but they did other damage that day. They took all the mules out of the lot and drove them away. They filled their "dugout wagons" with corn. A dugout wagon would hold nearly a crib full of corn. They were high in front and back and came down to a point, nearly touched the ground between the wheels. The wheels had pens instead of axles in them.

The children ran like pigs every morning. The pigs ran to eat acorns and the children—white and black—to pick up chestnuts, scaly barks and hickory nuts. There were lots of black walnuts. "We had barrels of nuts to eat all winter and the mistress sold some every year at Nashville, Tennessee. The woods were full of nut trees and we had a few maple and sweet gum trees. We simmered down maple sap for brown sugar and chewed the sweet gum. We picked up chips to simmer the sweet maple sap down. We used elder tree wood to make faucets for syrup barrels. There were chenquipins down in the swamps that the children gathered."

Henry Walker said that they were sent upon the hills to find ginsing and often found long beds of it. They put it in sacks and a man came and bought it from the mistress. The mistress' name was Mrs. Williams. She kept the money for the ginsing and nuts too when she sold them.

Henry said he ate at Mrs. Williams', but the other children ate at the cabin. On Saturday evening the horn would sound and every slave would come to get his allowance of provisions. They used a big bell hung up in a tree to call them to meals and to begin work. They could also hear other farm bells and horns. Colored folks could have dances if they would get permission. Some masters were overseers themselves and some hired overseers. Patty Rell was a white man and the bush-wackers give us trouble sometimes.

On January first every year everybody ate peas and "hog jole" and received the new rules. The masters would say, "don't be running up here telling me on the overseer." They had a bush harbor church and the white preacher came to preach to black and white sometimes. They taught obedience and the Golden Rules. No schools—Henry said since freedom the white men had cheated him out of all he had ever made, with pen-and-ink. He rather be whipped with a stick than a writing pen. He said Mr. and Mrs. Williams were good people. Henry learned to knit his socks and gloves at night watching the grown people. They made a certain number of broches every night. He liked that.

Henry said Mr. Williams let him carry his gun hunting with him and taught him how to shoot squirrels. They were plentiful. He had a lot of dogs. The master went to the deer stand and Henry managed the twelve hounds. He didn't like to fox hunt. About a hundred men and thirty dogs, horns, etc. out for the chase. They came from Nashville and in the country. A fox make three rounds from where he is jumped and then widens out. They brought "fine whiskey" out on the chases.

When they had corn shuckings one Negro would sit on the fence and lead the singing, the others shuck on each side. The master would pour out a tin cup full of whiskey from a big jug for each corn shucker, and Mrs. Williams would give each a square of gingerbread.

Mr. Williams set aside a certain number of acres of land every year to be cleared, fenced and broke for cultivation by spring. Six or eight men worked together. They used tong-hand sticks to carry the logs to the piles where they were burning them. A saw was a side show, they used mall, axe and wedge. After the log rolling there would be a big supper and a good one. The visitors got what they wanted from the table first. "That was manners."

"We took turns going to the Methodist church at Nashville with Mr. and Mrs. Williams. They went in the fine carriage and the maid held the baby but anybody else rode along behind on horseback. The carriage horses were curried every day, kept up and ate corn and fodder. Mr. and Mrs. Williams came to Nashville to big weddings and dances often."

After Henry Walker came to Hazen, Colonel Yopp had him feed his dogs and attend him on big fox hunting trips. Since Colonel Yopp died January 1928 Henry seldom, or perhaps has never sung the song he sang to Colonel for dimes if he needed a little change. He learned the song and whoop back in in slavery days. He said William Dorch (colored boy) took it up from hearing him sing for Colonel Yopp and would write it for me and sing it and give it with the old Carolina, Georgia and Tennessee whoop.

---

**Interviewer: Mrs. Bernice Bowden**
**Person interviewed: Jake Walker**
**3002 Short W. Ninth Avenue, Pine Bluff, Arkansas**
**Age: 95**

"Well, I was here"I was born in 1842, August the 4th. That makes me ninety-five in the clear. If I live till next August I'll be ninety-six.

"No ma'am, I wasn't born in Arkansas, I was born in Alabama. I been here in Arkansas bout forty or fifty years. I used to live in Mississippi when I first left the old country.

"Oh yes'm, I was bout big enough to go durin' the War, but I wouldn't run off. Couldn't a had no better master. That's the reason I'm livin' like I do. Always took good care of myself. Never had no exposure.

"I _did_ work fore the War, I'll say! Done anything they said.

"John Carmichael was my old master and Miss Nancy was old missis.

"Oh yes ma'am, I seed the Yankees. They stopped there. I wasn't askeered of nobody. I have went to the well and drawed water for em.

"I member when the War was gwine on. I didn't know why they was fightin'. If I did I done forgot"I'll be honest with you. I didn't know nothin' only they was fightin'. Most of my work was around the house. I never paid no tention to that war. I was livin' too fine them days. I was livin' a hundred days to the week. Yes ma'am, I did get along fine.

"Oh yes ma'am, I had good white folks. I never was sold. No ma'am, I born right on the old home place.

"Patrollers? Had to get a pass from your master to go over there. Oh yes, I know all about them. I have seed the Ku Klux too. Yes ma'am, I know all about them things.

"I never been to school but half a day. I went to work when I was eight years old and been workin' ever since.

"My father died in slave times and my mother died the fourth year after surrender.

"After freedom, I worked there bout the course of three or four years. Then I emigrated and come on to Mississippi. The most I done them times was farmin'. Reckon I stayed in Mississippi five or six years.

"The most work I done here in Arkansas is carpenter work. I'm the first colored man ever contracted in Pine Bluff.

"If I wasn't able to work, I don't think I'd stay here long.

"Used to drive the mule in the gin in slave times.

"We didn't have a bit of expense on us. Our doctor bills was paid and had clothes give to us and had plenty of something to eat.

"Yes'm, I used to vote but it's been for years since I voted. Voted Republican. I don't know why the colored people is Republican. You askin' me something now I don't know nothin' about, but I believe in votin' for the man goin' to do good"do the country good.

"Oh, don't talk about the younger generation"I jist can't accomplish em, I sure can't. They ain't got the 'regenious' and get-up about em they had in my time. They is more wiser, that's about all. The young race these days"I don't know what's gwine come of em. If twasn't for we old fogies, don't know what they'd do.

"We ain't never had that World War yet told about in the Bible. Called this last war the World War but twasn't.

"I've always tried to keep my place and I ain't never been in any kind of trouble."

**Interviewer: Miss Irene Robertson**
**Person interviewed: Jake Walker, Wheatley, Arkansas**
**Age: 68**

"I was born seven or eight miles from Hernando, Mississippi. My pa was a slave over twenty years. He belong to Master Will Walker, and his white mistress was Ann. They brought him from 'round Athens, Georgia. He was heired through his master. His own mother died at his birth and he was the son of a peddler through the country. He was a furriner but pa never could tell. His young master never told him. His ma was the nurse about the place. The peddler was a white man of some kind. He kept coming about selling goods. The dogs made a bad racket. They never bought nothing much. Old master suspicioned him trying to get away with something about the place. He come right out and accused him to being up to something. He denied it. He told the peddler not to come back. He never. After it was over she told her mistress. He wanted her to go on off with him. That made them mad. But he never was seen about there.

"When Will Walker got married he wanted my pa and he was give to him, a horse and buggy, two mules, a lamb, and five young cows. He had some money and he come to Mississippi. I reckon he did buy some land. He got to be a slave owner before freedom. Pa said he drove the horse to the buggy and his master rode a mule, led a mule and brought his cows, and they kept the lamb in the buggy with them nearly all the way.

"I think they was good to him. His young mistress cried so much they all went back once before freedom. They went on Christmas time. Only time he ever was drunk. He got down and nearly froze to death. The white folks heard he was somewhere down. They went and got him one Sunday morning in a two-horse wagon. He was nearly dead. That was his first and last spree.

"Pa said he nursed three of his young mistress' babies, Alfred, Tom, and Kenneth.

"After freedom pa went to Texas with Alfred Walker. He owned a ranch out on the desert and raised Texas ponies and big horn cows. They sent a carload of young cattle to St. Louis and pa stopped back in Mississippi and married ma. She was a Walker too, Libbie Walker. There was fourteen of us children. They nearly all went to Louisiana to work in the timber. I come to Clarendon. I been married three times. My last wife left me and took my onliest child. Only child I ever had. They was at Hot Springs last account I had of them. She was cooking for a woman over there. My girl is up 'bout grown now. She come to Clarendon to see me three years ago. I sent for her but she wouldn't stay. She writes to me, but I have to get somebody to write for me and somebody to read her letters. I can read print real good. I never went to school a day in my whole life. We had to work early and late when I come up.

"I farmed, sawmilled, worked in the timber. I do public work, haul wood, cut wood, and work in the field by day labor.

"I votes a Republican ticket. I haven't voted since Mr. Taft run. I don't have no way to keep up with elections now. Folks used to talk more, now they keeps quiet.

"I never heard pa say how he come to know about freedom. Ma said she was refugeed to Texas and when they brung them back, Master Will Walker met them at the creek on his place and he said, 'You all are free now. You can go on my place or hunt other places.' They went on his place and they lived there a long time. I don't remember ever living on that place. Pa wasn't there then. I don't know where be could been. Ma and pa was both Walkers but no blood kin. Ma didn't talk much about old times. She was sold once, she said. Bass Kelly bought her. I don't know if Will Walker traded for her. She never did say. Bass Kelly was mean to her. He beat her and one time she hid and kept hid till she nearly starved, she said. She hid in the corn crib. It was a log house. She didn't enjoy slavery. Pa had a very good time, better than us boys had it when we come up. He worked and kept us with him. He and ma died the same week. They had pneumonia in Mississippi.

"I got one sister. She lives close to Shreveport. She keeps up with us all. I go down there every now and then. She's not stove up like I am. She wants me to stay with her all the time. I gets work down there easier but I have the rheumatism bad down there.

"I don't know what will become of young folks. I wish I had their chance. They can't wait for nothing. They in too big a hurry for the crop to grow. Busy living by the day. When the year gone they ain't no better off. Times is good in places. Hard in places. Times better in Louisiana than up here. Work easier to get. Folks got more living.

"I'm chopping cotton on Mr. Hill's place. I gets ninety cents a day. I can't get over the ground fast."

---

**Interviewer: Bernice Bowden**
**Person interviewed: Willie Wallace**
**40th and Georgia Streets, Pine Bluff, Arkansas**
 **Age: 80**

"I was born in Green County, Alabama. Elihu Steele was my old master. Miss Julia was old missis. She was Elihu's wife. Her mother's name was Penny Hatter. Miss Penny give my mother to her daughter Julia.

"I was a twin and they choosed us for the cook and washer and ironer, but surrender come along 'fore we got big enough to do anything.

"My father was crippled and couldn't work in the field, and I remember he used to carry the children out to the field to be suckled.

"They had a right smart of slaves. My mother had twelve children and I'm the baby.

"I remember they'd make up a big pot of corn bread and pot-liquor and they'd say, 'Eat, chillun, eat.'

"I remember one time the white folks had some stock tied out, and I know my sister's little boy didn't know no better and he showed the Yankees where they was.

"I remember when they said the people was free, but our folks stayed right on there—I don't know how many years—'cause my mother thought a heap of her old missis, Penny.

"I went to school after freedom and learned how to read and write and figger. I worked in the field till I got disabled. I never did wash and iron and cook for the white folks.

"I was fifteen—somewhere in there—when I married and I'm the mother of twelve children.

"I have lived in Thomas, West Virginia; Pittsburg, Pennsylvania; Cumberland, Maryland; Milliken, Louisiana; and Birmingham, Alabama. I just lived in all them places following my children around.

"I fell through a trestle in Birmingham and injured myself comin' from church.

"I think the people is gettin' terrible now. You think they're gettin' better? I think they're gettin' wuss.

"I got a book here called 'Uncle Tom' and I hates to read it sometimes 'cause the people suffered so.

"I don't think old master had any overseers. Miss Julia wouldn't 'low any of her people to be beat."

---

**Interviewer: Mrs. Bernice Bowden**
**Person interviewed: Evans Warrior**
**609 E. 23rd Avenue, Pine Bluff, Arkansas**
  **Age: 80**

"I was born here in Arkansas in Dallas County. I don't know zackly what year but I was bout five when they drove us to Texas. Stayed there three years till the war ceasted.

"Old master's name was Nat Smith. He was good to me. I was big enough to plow same year the war ceasted.

"Yankees come through Texas after peace was 'clared. They'd come by and ask my mother for bread. She was the cook.

"We left Arkansas 'fore the war got busy. Everything was pretty ragged after we got back. White folks was here but colored folks was scattered. My folks come back and went to their native home in Dallas County.

"Never did nothin' but farm work. Worked on the shares till I got able to rent. Paid five or six dollars a acre. Made some money.

"I heered of the Ku Klux. Some of em come through the Clemmons place and put notice on the doors. Say VACATE. All the women folks got in one house. Then the boss man come down and say there wasn't nothin' to it. Boss man didn't want em there.

"I went to school a little. Kep' me in the field all the tims. Didn't get fur enuf to read and write.

"Yes'm, I voted. Voted the Republican ticket. That's what they give me to vote. I couldn't read so I'd tell em who I wanted to vote for and they'd put it down. Some of my friends was justice of the peace and constables.

"I been in Pine Bluff bout four years—till I got disabled to work.

"I been married five times. All dead but two. Don't know how many chillun we had—have to go back and study over it.

"Some of the younger generation is out of reason. Ain't strict on chillun now like the old folks was."

**Interviewer: Miss Irene Robertson**
**Person interviewed: Anna Washington, Clarendon, Arkansas**
**(Back of Mrs. Maynard's home in the alley)**
 **Age: 77**

"I've forgot who my mother's owner was. She was born in Virginia. She was put on a block and sold. She was fifteen years old and she never seen her mother again after she left her. Her master was George Birdsong. He bought my papa too. They was onliest two he owned. He wanted them both light so the children would be light for house girls and waiting boys. Light colored folks sold for more money on the block.

"The boss man over grandpa and grandma in Virginia was John Glover. But he was not their owner. My grandpa was about white. He said his owners was good to him but now grandma had a pided back where she had been whooped. Grandpa come down from the Washington slaves so my papa said. That is the reason I holds to his name and my boy holds to it. Papa said he had to plough and clean up new ground for Master Birdsong. He was a young man starting out and papa and mama was young too.

(She left and came back with some old scraps of yellow and torn papers dimly written all over: Anna Washington, born 1860 at Hines County at Big Rock. Mother born at Capier County. Father born at White County, Virginia—ed.)

"This is what was told to me by my papa: His grandmother was born of George Washington's housemaid. That was one hundred forty years ago. His papa was educated under a fine mechanic and he help build the old State-house at Washington. Major Rousy Paten was the Washington nigger 'ministrator.

"I had a sister named Martha Curtis after his young wife. I had a brother named Housy Patton. They are both dead now. Pa lived to be ninety-eight years old. My mama was as white as you is but she was a nigger woman. Pa was lighter than I is now. I'm getting darker 'cause I'm getting old. My pa was named Benjamin Washington.

"I heard my pa talk about Nat Turner. (She knew who he was o.k.—ed.) He got up a rebellion of black folk back in Virginia. I heard my pa sit and tell about him. Moses Kinnel was a rich white man wouldn't sell Nellie 'cause of what his wife said. She was a housemaid. He wrote own free pass book and took her to Maryland. Father's father wanted to buy Nellie but her owner wouldn't sell her. He took her.

"My mother had fourteen children. We and Archie was the youngest.

"Moses Kinnel was a rich white man and had lots of servants. He promised never to sell Nellie and keep her to raise his white children. She was his maid. He promised that her dying bed. But father's father stole her and took her to Maryland.

"Pa run away and was sold twice or more. When he was small chile his mother done fine washing. She seat him to go fetch her some fine laundry soap what they bought in the towns. Two white men in a two-wheel open buggy say, 'Hey, don't you want to ride?' 'I ain't got time.' 'Get in buggy, we'll take you a little piece.' One jumped out and tied his hands together. They sold him. They let him go to nigger traders. They had him at a doctor's examining his fine head see what he could stand. The doctor say, 'He is a fine man. Could trust him with silver and gold—his weight in it.' They brung him to Mississippi and sold him for a big price. He had these papers the doctor wrote on him to show.

"Then he sent for my mama after they sat him free. His name was Ben Washington.

"He never spoke much of freedom. He said his master in Mississippi told them and had them sign up contracts to finish that year's crop. He took back his old Virginia name and I don't recollect that master's name. Heard it too. Yes ma'am, heap er times. My recollection is purty nigh gone.

"I don't get no younger in feelings 'cause I'm getting old."

---

**FOLKLORE SUBJECTS**
**Interviewer: S.S. Taylor**
**Subject: Slave memories—Birth, Mother, Father, Separation House**
**Subject: Slaves—Dwellings, Food, Clothes**
**Subject: Corn Shucking, Dances, Quiltings, Weddings among Slaves**
**Subject: Slaves—Fight with Master (junior); Slave uprisings**
**Subject: Confederate Army Negroes; Ex-slave Occupations**
**Story:—Information**

**This information given by: Eliza Washington**
**Place of Residence: 1517 West Seventeenth**
**Little Rock, Arkansas**
**Occupation: Washing and Ironing (When able)**
**Age: About 77**

[TR: Information moved from bottom of first page.]
[TR: Repetitive information deleted from subsequent pages.]

The first thing I remember was living with my mother about six miles from Scott's Crossing in Arkansas, about the year 1866. I know it was 1866 because it was the year after the surrender, and we know the surrender was in 1865. I know the dates after 1866. You don't know nothin' when you don't know dates. If you get up in court and say somethin', the lawyers ask you when it happened and then they ask you where did it happen, and if you can't tell them, they say "Witness is excused. You don't know nothin'."

## Mother and Father

My mother was born in North Carolina in Mecklinberg in Henderson County. I don't know when she came to Arkansas, and I don't know when she went to Tennessee.

My father was born in Tennessee. I don't know the county like I did in North Carolina. I don't know the town either, but I think it was in the rurals somewhere. The white folks separated my mother and father when I was a little baby in their arms. The people to whom my father belonged stayed in Tennessee, but my mother's people came to Arkansas. It must have been along in the time of the war that they come to Arkansas.

## Dwelling

My mother lived in a log house chinked with wood chinks. The chinks looked like gluts. You know what a glut is? No? Well a glut looks like the pattern of a shoe. They lay the logs together, and then chink up the cracks with wood blocks made up like the pattern of a shoe. These were chinks, wooden things about a foot long, shaped like a wedge. They were used for chinking. After the logs were laid together, chinks would be needed to stop up the holes between the logs. After the chinking was finished, clay was stuffed in to stop up the cracks and make the house warm. I've seen a many a one built.

Wide planks were used for the floors. The doors were hung on wooden hinges. The doors were never locked. They didn't have any looks on them. You could bar them on the inside if you wanted to. They didn't have no fear of burglars in them days. People wasn't bad then as they is now. They had just one window and one door in the house. The chimney was built up like a ladder and clay and straw was stuffed in the framework.

I have seen such houses built right down here in Scott's. My mother was a field hand. She lived in such a house in Tennessee. There wasn't no brick about the house, not even in the chimney. In later years, they have covered up all those logs with weather boards and made the houses look like what they call "modern", but theyr'e the same old log houses.

## Food

My mother said her white folks fed her well. She had whatever they had. When she came to Arkansas, they issued rations, but she never was issued rations before. When they issued rations, they gave them so much food each week—so much corn meal, so much potatoes, so much cabbage, so much molasses, so much meat—mostly rubbish-like food. We went out in the garden and dug the potatoes and got the cabbage.

But in Tennessee, my mother got what ever she wanted whenever she wanted it. If she wanted salt, she went and got it. If she wanted meat, she went to the smokehouse and got it. Whatever she wanted, she went and got it, and they didn't have no times for issuing out.

## Social Affairs—Corn Shuckings, Quiltings and Dances

The biggest time I remember on the plantations was corn shucking time. Plenty of corn was brought in from the cribs and strowed along where everybody could get to it freely. Then they would all get corn and shuck it until near time to quit. The corn shucking was always at night, and only as much corn as they thought would be shucked was brought from the cribs. Just before they got through, they would begin to sing. Some of the songs were pitiful and sad. I can't remember any of them, but I can remember that they were sad. One of them began like this:

"The speculator bought my wife and child
 And carried her clear away."

When they got through shucking, they would hunt up the boss. He would run away and hide just before. If they found him, two big men would take him up on their shoulders and carry him all around the grounds while they sang. My mother told me that they used to do it that way in slave time.

## Dances

They didn't dance then like they do now all hugged up and indecent. In them days, they danced what you call square dances. They don't do those dances now, they're too decent. There were eight on a set. I used to dance those myself.

## Quiltings

I heard mother say she went to a lot of quiltings. I suppose they had them much the same as they do now. Everybody took a part of the quilt to finish. They talked and sang and had a good time. And they had somethin' to eat at the close just as they did in the corn shucking. I never went to a quilting.

## Worship

Some of the Niggers went to church then just as they do now, and some of them weren't allowed to go.

Reverend Winfield used to preach to the colored people that if they would be good niggers and not steal their master's eggs and chickens and things, that they might go to the kitchen of heaven when they died.

An old lady once said to me, "I would give anything if I could have Maria in heaven with me to do little things for me." My mother told me that the niggers had to turn the pots down to keep their voices from sounding when they were praying at night. And they couldn't sing at all.

## Weddings

I can remember that they used to have weddings when I was a child around the years 1867 and 1868. My mother told me of marriages and weddings. She never saw no paint on anybody's face. They used to have powder, but they never used any paint. Girls were better then than they are now.

## Fight with Master

My mother's first master was named Rasly, and her second was named Neely. She and her young master, John McNeely, who was raised with her and who was about the same age as she was, got to fighting one day and she whipped him clear as a whistle. After she whipped him that fight went all over the country. She was between sixteen and seventeen years old an he was about the same. She had never been whipped by the white folks.

She was in the kitchen. I don't know what the trouble started over. But they had an argument. There were some other white boys in the kitchen with her young master, and they kept pushing the two of them up to fight. He wanted to show off; so he told her what he would do to her if she didn't hush her mouth. She told him to just try it, and the fight was on. So they fought for about an hour, and the other white boys egged them on.

She said that her old master never did whip her, and she sure wasn't going to let the young one do it. I never heard that they punished her for whipping her young master. I never heard her say that anybody tried to whip her at any other time. My mother was a strong woman. She could lift one end of a log with any man.

## Slave Uprisings

My mother used to say that when she was about fourteen years old, (That was about the time that the stars fell, and the stars fell in 1833 [HW:*]. So she must have been born in 1819. In 1833, she was sold for a fourteen year old girl. That was the only time that she ever was sold. That left her about eighty-three years old when she died in 1903.) She used to say that when she was about fourteen years old, and was living in North Carolina in Mecklinburg Co, in Henderson County, that the white folks called all the slaves up to the big house and kept them there a few days. There wasn't no trouble on my mother's place, but they had heard that there was an uprising among the slaves, and they called all the Niggers up to the house. They didn't do nothin' to them. They just called them up to the house, and kept them there. It all passed over soon. I don't know nothin' else about it.

## Confederate Army Negroes

I've "heered" old Brother Zachary who used to belong to Bethel Church tell about the surrender. Brother Zachary is dead now. He was a soldier In the Confederate army. He fought all through the war and he used to tell lots of stories about it.

You know, Lee was a tall man, fine looking and dignified. Grant was a little man and short. Those two generals walked up to each other with a white flag in their hands. And they talked and agreed just when they would fight. And then they both went back to their armies, and they fought the awfulest battle you ever "heered" of. The men lay dead in rows and rows and rows. The dead men covered whole fields. And General Lee said that there wasn't any use doing any more fighting. General Grant let all the rebels keep their guns. He didn't take nothin' away from them.

I saw General Grant when he came to Little Rock. There was an old white man who had never been to Little Rock in his life. He said "I just had to come up here to see this great general that they are talking about."

## Occupations

We always worked in the field in slave time. I don't know nothin about share cropping because I always did days work. I used to get four and five dollars a week for washing. But now they wants the young folks and they don't pay them five dollars for everything. I can't get a pension. Why you reckon they won't give me one. They don't understand that that little house I own doesn't even keep itself up. My daughter-in-law is good to me but she needs everything she makes. I can't get much to do now, and what little I gets, they don't pay me much for.

I don' remember nothin' else.

**Interviewer: Miss Irene Robertson**
**Person interviewed: Jennie Washington, DeValls Bluff, Arkansas**
**Age: 80**

"My mother was a slave and my father too I recken. They belonged to Jack Walton when I remembered. I was born at St. Charles. My mother died in time of the war at St. Louis. This is whut I remembers. My mother was sold twice. The Prices owned her and the Wakefields owned her before she was owned by old Jack Walton. I was the youngest child. I had one brother went to war and he drawed a pension long as he lived. We children all got scattered out. Mr. Walton bout the age of my father and he said some day all these niggers be set free and warnt long fore they sho was. I had one older sister I recollect mighty well. My mother named Fannie, my father named Abe Walton. He had a young master James Walton.

"When I was nuthin but a chile I remembers James dressed up like Ku Klux Klan and scared me. The old master sho did whoop him bout that. They take care of the little black children and feed em good an don't let em do too hard er work to stunt em so they take em off and sell em for a good price.

"I remembers the little old log house my granma and granpa way back over on the place stayed in till they died. We went back after the war and lived ten years on the same place. We lived close to the white folks in a bigger house.

"I don't recollect no big change after freedom cept they quit selling and working folks without giving them money. I was too small to notice much change then I speck. Times has always been tight wid me. I ain't never had very much. I did work an a livin is all I ever got out of it. Never could make enough to get ahead.

"The white folks never give the darky nothing when freedom declared. We used to raise tobacco and sell it to smoke and make snuff. And he had em make ax handles to sell on the side for money till the crops gathered.

"If you believe in the Bible you won't believe in women votin' I never did vote. I ain't goner never vote.

"The present condition is fine. Mrs. Robinson carries a great big truck load to her farm every day to pick cotton. She sent word up here she take anybody whut wanter work. I wish I was able to go. I loves to pick cotton. She pay em seventy-five cents a hundred. She'll pay em too! I don't know what they do this winter. Set by the fire I recken. But next spring she'll let hoe that crop. She took em this past year to hoe out that very cotton they pickin now. Her husband, he's sick. He keeps their store up town. She takes a few white hands too if they wanter work. I don't think the present generation no worse en they ever been. They drawed up closer together than they used to be. They buys everything now an they don't raise nuthin. It's the Bible fulfillin. Everything so high they caint save nuthin!

"I married twice. First time in the church, other time at home. I had four children. I had two in Detroit. I don't know where my son is. He may be there yet. My daughter there got fourteen children her own. I don't know where the others are. Nom [TR: long "o" diacritical] they don't help me a bit, do well helpin theirselves. I gets the Welfare sistance and I works my garden back here."

---

**Interviewer: Mrs. Bernice Bowden**
**Person interviewed: Parrish Washington**
**812 Spruce Street, Pine Bluff, Arkansas**
**Age: 86**

"I was born in 1852—born in Arkansas. Sam Warren was my old master.

"I remember some of the Rebel generals—General Price and General Marmaduke.

"We had started to Texas but the Yankees got in ahead of us in the Saline bottoms and we couldn't go no further.

"My boss had so much faith in his own folks he wouldn't leave here 'til it was too late. He left home on Saturday night and got into the bottoms on Sunday and made camp. Then the Yankees got in ahead of him and he couldn't go no further, so we come back to Jefferson County.

"The Yankees had done took Little Rock and come down to Pine Bluff.

"My father died in 1860 and my mother in 1865.

"I can remember when they whipped the slaves. Never whipped me though— they was just trainin' me up.

"Had an old lady on the place cooked for the children and we just got what we could.

"I remember when peace was declared, the people shouted and rejoiced—a heavy load had fell off.

"All the old hands stayed on the place. I stayed there with my uncle and aunt. We was treated better then. I was about 25 years old when I left there.

"I farmed 'til '87. Then I joined the Conference and preached nearly forty years when I was superannuated.

"I remember when the Rebels was camped up there on my boss's place. I used to love to see the soldiers. Used to see the horses hitched to the artillery.

"Two or three of Sam Warren's hands run off and joined the Yankees. They didn't know what it was goin' to be and two of 'em come back—stayed there too.

"I used to vote the Republican ticket. I was justice of the peace four years—two terms.

"I went to school here in Pine Bluff about two or three terms and I was school director in district number two about six or seven years.

"I have great hope for the young people of the future. 'Course some of 'em are not worth killin' but the better class—I think there is a bright future for 'em.

"But for the world in general, if they don't change they goin' to the devil. But God always goin' to have some good people in reserve 'til the Judgment."

---

**Interviewer: Mrs. Bernice Bowden**
**Person interviewed: Caroline Watson**
**517 E. 21st Avenue, Pine Bluff, Arkansas**
**Age: 82**

"I was born in '55 in March on the 13th on Sunday morning in time for breakfast. I was born in Mississippi. I never will forget my white folks. Oh, I was raised good. I had good white folks. Wish I could see some of em now.

"Well, I specs I do remember when the war started. I member when twas goin' on. Oh Lord, I member all bout it. Old mistress' name was Miss Ellen Shird.

"Oh the Yankees used to come around. I can see us chillun sittin' on the gallery watchin' em. I disremember what color uniform they had on, but I seen a heap of em.

"My old master, I can see him now—old Joe Shird. Just as good as they could be.

"I should say I do remember when they surrendered. I know everybody was joyous. But they done better fore surrender than they did afterwards—that is them that had to go off to themselves.

"I was always so fast tryin' to work I wasn't studyin' bout no books, but I went to school after surrender. My father and mother was smart old folks and made us work.

"I just been married once. I did pretty well. I like to been married since he's dead but I seen so many didn't do so well. I has four sons and one daughter. My son made me quit workin'. They gets me anything I want. I got a religion that will do to die with. I done give up everything.

"Younger generation? What we goin' do with em? They ought to be sent off some place and put to work. They just gone to the dogs. The Lord have mercy. My heart just aches and moans and groans for em."

---

STATE—Arkansas
NAME OF WORKER—Samuel S. Taylor
ADDRESS—Little Rock, Arkansas
DATE—December, 1938
SUBJECT—Ex-slave

[TR: Repetitive information deleted from subsequent pages.]

## Circumstances of Interview

1. Name and address of informant—**Mary Watson**, 1500 Cross Street, Little Rock.

2. Date and time of interview—

3. Place of interview—1500 Cross Street, Little Rock.

4. Name and address of person, if any, who put you in touch with informant—

5. Name and address of person, if any, accompanying you—

6. Description of room, house, surroundings, etc.—

## Personal History of Informant

1. Ancestry—father, Abram McCoy; mother, Louise McCoy.

2. Place and date of birth—Mississippi. No date.

3. Family—

4. Places lived in, with dates—Lived in Mississippi until 1891 then moved to Arkansas.

5. Education, with dates—

6. Occupations and accomplishments, with dates—

7. Special skills and interests—

8. Community and religious activities—

9. Description of informant—

10. Other points gained in interview—This person tells very little of life, but tells of her parents.

## Text of Interview (Unedited)

"My mother and father were McCoys. His name was Abram and her name was Louise. My mother died right here when Brewer was Pastor of Wesley. You ought to remember her. My mother died in 1928. My father died in 1897 when Joe Sherrill was pastor. Joe Sherrill went to Africa, you know. He was a missionary.

"My mother was owned by Bill Mitchell. He came from Alabama. I can't call the name of the town, just now. Yes, I can; it was Tuscaloosa. My father came from South Carolina. McCoy was his owner. But how come him to leave South Carolina he was sold after his master died and the property was divided. He was sold away from his family. He had a large family—about nine children. My mother was sold away from her mother too. She was little and couldn't help herself. My grandma didn't want to come. And she managed not to; I don't know how she managed it.

"Before freedom my father was a farmer. My mother was a farmer too. My mother wasn't so badly treated. She was a slave but she worked right along with the white children. She had two brothers. The other sister stayed with her mother. She was sold—my mother's mother. But I don't know to whom.

"My father was a preacher. He could word any hymn. How could he do it, I don't know. On his Sunday, when the circuit rider wasn't there, he would have me read the Bible to him and then he could get up and tell it to the people. I don't know how he managed it. He didn't know how to read. But he had a wonderful memory. He always had his exhorting license renewed and he exhorted the people both Methodists and Baptists. After freedom, when I went to school I knew and always helped him.

"My father voted on the election days all the time. Be was a Republican, and he rallied to them all the time. Before the war, my father farmed. He commenced in the early fall hauling the cotton from Abbeville, South Carolina to Augusta, Georgia. That was his business—teamster, hauling cotton. He never did talk like his owners were so mean to him. Of course, they weren't mean. When her master died and the property had to be sold, his master bought her and her babies.

"My father met my mother before the war started. Colored people were scarce in the locality where she lived. These white people saw my father and liked him. And they encouraged her to marry him. She was only seventeen. My father was much older. He remembered the dark day in May and when the stars fell.

"He didn't show his age much though till he came to Little Rock. He had been used to farming and city life didn't agree with him. He left about seven years after coming here.

"My father and mother met and married in Mississippi. He came from South Carolina and she came from Alabama. They had nine children. All of them were born after the war. I am the oldest. Lee McCoy is my youngest brother. You know him, I'm sure. He is the president of Rust College. I was born right after the war. Don't put me down as no ex-slave. I was born right after the war.

"Right after the war, my father farmed in Mississippi. He took a notion to come to Arkansas in 1891. He brought his whole family with him. And I have been out here ever since.

"I never saw any slave houses. I wasn't a slave. I have been to the place where my mother was raised. I was teaching school near there and just wanted to see. After her master died, Sam McCallister, his cousin, took the slave children and was their guardian. Years later it come up in court and they took all his land. Bill Mitchell was her first master. He died during slave time. McCallister was made administrator of the estate. He was made guardian of all the children too. He was made guardian of the white children and of the colored children. He raised them all. There was Ma and her auntie and three or four children of her auntie's. Later on, way after the war, there was a lawsuit. I was grown then. The courts made him pay the white children their share as far as he was able. Of course, the colored children got nothing because they were slaves when he took them.

"I don't know nothing about the Ku Klux Klan bothering my family. I don't remember anything except that I hear them talking about the Ku Klux and the Pateroles. I wasn't here.

"Don't put me down as an ex-slave. I am not an ex-slave. I was born after the war. I don't know nothing about slavery except what I heard others say. I expect I have talked too much anyway."

**Extra Comment**

The constant reiteration of the phrase, "I'm not an ex-slave" roused my curiosity and drove me to a superficial investigation. Persons who are acquainted with her and her family estimate that Mary Watson is nearer eighty than seventy. She started her story pleasantly enough. But when she got the obsession that she would be put down as an ex-slave, she refused to tell more.

There is one thing not to be overlooked. Mary Watson has a mind that is still keen. She tells what she wants to tell, and she doesn't state a thing that she does not want to state. The hidden facts are to be discerned only by subtle inference.

This trait interested me, for her younger brother, mentioned in the story, is a distinguished character, President of Rust College, Holly Springs, Mississippi, and known to be experienced and efficient in his work. Whatever she may have reserved or stated, in reading her story, we are reading at least a sidelight on a family of which some of the members have done some fine work within the race.

---

**Interviewer: Miss Irene Robertson**
**Person interviewed: Person interviewed: Bart Wayne,**
**Helena,Arkansas**
**Age: 72**

"I was born at Holly Springs in 1866. It was in the springtime. Ma said I was born two years after the surrender. Ma was named Mary and pa Dan—Dan Wayne. They never was sold. In 1912 Dr. Leard was living in a big fine house at Sardia, Mississippi. He was our last owner. Mallard Jones owned them too. Pa didn't have no name. He was called for his owners. I don't know if he named hisself Dan Wayne or not. The way I think it was, Mr. Jones give Dr. Leard's wife them. He give her a big plantation. I knowed Dr. Leard my own self all my life. I'd go to see him.

"The present times is hard. I get ten dollars a month. I don't know what to say about folks now—none of them."

---

**Interviewer: Pernella Anderson**
**Person interviewed: Annie Mae Weathers**
**East Bone Street**
**El Dorado, Ark.**
**Age: ?**

"I was born bout the second year after surrender right down here at Caledonia. Now the white folks that ma and pa and me belonged to was named Fords. We farmed all the time. The reason we farmed all the time was because that was all for us to do. You see there wasn't nothin' else for us to do. There wasn't no schools in my young days to do no good, and this time of year we was plowin' to beat the band and us always planted corn in February and in April our corn was.

"We fixed our ground early and planted early and we had good crops of everything. We went to bed early and rose early. We had a little song that went like this:

Early to bed and early to rise
Makes a man healthy, wealthy, and wise.
and
The early bird catches the worm.

Cooked breakfast every morning by a pine torch.

"I member hearin' my pa say that when somebody come and hollowed: 'Yer niggers is free at last' say he just dropped his hoe and said in a queer voice: 'Thank God for that.' It made old miss and old moss so sick till they stopped eating a week. Pa said old moss and old miss looked like their stomach and guts had a law suit and their navel was called in for a witness, they was so sorry we was free.

"After I got a good big girl I was hired out for my clothes and something to eat. My dresses was made out of cotton stripes and my chemise was made out of flannelette and my under pants was made out of homespun.

"Our games was 'Honey, honey Bee,' 'Ball I can't Yall,' and a nother one of our games was 'Old Lady Hypocrit.'"

**Interviewer: Samuel S. Taylor**
**Person interviewed: Cora Weathers**
**818 Chester Street, Little Rock, Arkansas**
**Age: 79**

"I have been right on this spot for sixty-three years. I married when I was sixteen and he brought me here and put me down and I have been here ever since. No, I don't mean he deserted me; I mean he put me on this spot of ground. Of course, I have been away on a visit but I haven't been nowheres else to live.

"When I came here, there was only three houses—George Winstead lived on Chester and Eighth Street; Dave Davis lived on Ninth and Ringo; and George Gray lived on Chester and Eighth. Rena Lee lived next to where old man Paterson stays now, 906 Chester. Rena Thompson lived on Chester and Tenth. The old people that used to live here is mostly dead or moved up North.

"On Seventh and Ringo there was a little store. It was the only store this side of Main Street. There was a little old house where Coffin's Drug Store is now. The branch ran across there. Old man John Peyton had a nursery in a little log house. You couldn't see it for the trees. He kept a nursery for flowers. On the next corner, old man Sinclair lived. That is the southeast corner of Ninth and Broadway. Next to him was the Hall of the Sons of Ham.

"That was the first place I went to school. Lottie Stephens, Robert Lacy, and Gus Richmond were the teacher. Hollins was the principal. That was in the Sons of Ham's Hall.

"I was born in Dallas County, Arkansas. It must have been 'long 'bout in eighty-fifty-nine, 'cause I was sixteen years old when I come here and I been here sixty-three years.

"During the War, I was quite small. My mother brought me here after the War and I went to school for a while. Mother had a large family. So I never got to go to school but three months at a time and only got one dollar and twenty-five cents a week wages when I was working. My father drove a wagon and hoed cotton. Mother kept house. She had—lemme see—one, two, three, four—eight of us, but the youngest brother was born here.

"My mother's name was Millie Stokes. My mother's name before she was married was—I don't know what. My father's name was William Stokes. My father said he was born in Maryland. I met Richard Weathers here and married him sixty-three years ago. I had six children, three girls and three boys. Children make you smart and industrious—make you think and make you get about.

"I've heard talk of the pateroles; they used to whip the slaves that was out without passes, but none of them never bothered us. I don't remember anything myself, because I was too small. I heard of the Ku Klux too; they never bothered my people none. They scared the niggers at night. I never saw none of them. I can't remember how freedom came. First I knowed, I was free.

"People in them days didn't know as much as the young people do now. But they thought more. Young people nowadays don't think. Some of them will do pretty well, but some of them ain't goin' to do nothin'. They are gittin' worse and worser. I don't know what is goin' to become of them. They been dependin' on the white folks all along, but the white folks ain't sayin' much now. My people don't seem to want nothin'. The majority of them just want to dress and run up and down the streets and play cards and policy and drink and dance. It is nice to have a good time but there is something else to be thought of. But if one tries to do somethin', the rest tries to pull him down. The more education they get, the worse they are—that is, some of them."

---

**Interviewer: Samuel S. Taylor**
**Person interviewed: Ishe Webb**
**1610 Cross Street, Little Rock, Arkansas**
**Age: 78, or more**

"I was born October 14. That was in slavery time. The record is burnt up. I was born in Atlanta, Georgia. My father's master was a Webb. His first name was

Huel. My father was named after him. I came here in 1874, and I was a boy eleven or twelve years old then.

"My father was sold to another man for seventeen hundred dollars. My mother was sold for twenty hundred. I have heard them say that so much that I never will forget it. Webb sold my father and bought him back. My mother's folks were Calverts. The Calverts and the Webbs owned adjoining plantations.

"My grandmother on my mother's side was a Calvert too. Her first name was Joanna. I think my father's parents got beat to death in slavery. Grandfather on my mother's side was tied to a stump and whipped to death. He was double jointed and no two men could whip him. They wanted to whip him because he wouldn't work. That was what they would whip any one for. They would run off before they would work. Stay in the woods all night.

"My Grandma Calvert was buried over here in Galloway on the Rock Island road on the John Eynes plantation.

"My folks' masters were all right. But them nigger drivers were bad, just like the county farm. A man sitting in the house and putting you over a lot of men, you gwinter go up high as you want to.

"My father was a blacksmith and my mother was a weaver. There was a lot of those slavery folks 'round the house, and they tell me they didn't work them till they were twenty-one, they put them in the field when they were twenty-two. If you didn't work they would beat you to death. My father killed his overseer and went on off to the War.

"The pateroles used to drive and whip them. They would catch the slaves off without a pass and whip them and then make the boss pay for them when they took them back. I never seen the pateroles but I have seen the Ku Klux and they were the same thing.

"The jayhawkers would catch you when the pateroles didn't. They would carry you to the pateroles and get pay for you, and the pateroles would turn you over to the owners. You had to have a pass. If you didn't the pateroles would catch you and wear you out, keep you till the next morning, and then send you home by the jayhawkers. They didn't call them that though, they called them bushwhackers.

"The Ku Klux came after the War. They was the same thing as the pateroles—they come out from them. I know where the Ku Klux home is over here on Eighteenth and Broadway. That is where they broke up. It ain't never been open since. (Not correct—ed.)

"I saw the Yankees come in the yard on the Webb place. That was in the time of the War. The old man got on his horse and flew. The Yankees went in the smokehouse, broke it open, got all the meat they wanted. They didn't pay you nothing in slavery time. But what meat the Yankees didn't take for themselves, they give to the niggers.

"My folks never got anything for their work that I know of. I heard my mother say that nobody got paid for their work. I don't know whether they had a chance to make anything on the side or not.

"The Yankees, when they come in the yard that morning, told my father he was free. I remember that myself. They come up riding horses and carryin' long old guns with bayonets on them, and told him. They rode all over the country from one place to another telling the niggers they were free. Master didn't get a chance to tell us because he left when he saw them comin'.

"When my mother and father were living on the plantation, they lived in an old frame building. A portion of it was log. My father stayed with the Calverts—his wife's white folks. At first old man Webb sold him to them; then he bought him back and bought my mother too. They were together when freedom came. You know they auctioned you off in slavery time. Every year, they would, they put you up on the auction block and buy and sell. That was down in Georgia. We was in Georgia when we was freed—in Atlanta. My father and mother had fourteen children altogether. My mother died the year after we came out here. That would be about 1875. I never had but three children because my wife died early. Two of them are dead.

"Right after freedom, my father plaited baskets and mats. He shucked mops, put handles on rakes and did things like that in addition to his farming. He was a

77

blacksmith all the time too. He used to plait collars for mules. He farmed and got his harvests in season. The other things would be a help to him between times.

"My father came here because he thought that there was a better situation here than in Georgia. Of course, the living was better there because they had plenty of fruit. Then he worked on a third and fourth. He got one bale of cotton out of every three he made. The slaves left many a plantation and they would grow up in weeds. When a man would clear up the ground like this and plant it down in something, he would get all he planted on it. That was in addition to the ground that he would contract to plant. He used to plant rice, peas, potatoes, corn, and anything else he wanted too. It was all his'n so long as it was on extra ground he cleared up.

"But they said, 'Cotton grows as high as a man in Arkansas.' Then they paid a man two dollars fifty cents for picking cotton here in Arkansas while they just paid about forty cents in Georgia. So my father came here. Times was good when we come here. The old man cleared five bales of cotton for himself his first year, and he raised his own corn. He bought a pony and a cow and a breeding hog out of the first year's money. He died about thirty-five years ago.

"When I was coming along I did public work after I became a grown man. First year I made crops with him and cleared two bales for myself at twelve and a half cents a pound. The second year I hired out by the month at forty-five dollars per month and board. I had to buy my clothes of course. After seven years I went to doing work as a millwright here in Arkansas. I stayed at that eighteen months. Then I steamboated.

"We had a captain on that steamboat that never called any man by his name. We rolled cotton down the hill to the boat and loaded it on, and if you weren't a good man, that cotton got wet. I never wetted my cotton. But jus' the same, I heard what the others heard. One day after we had finished loading, I thought I'd tell him something. The men advised me not to. He was a rough man, and he carried a gun in his pocket and a gun in his shirt. I walked up to him and said, 'Captain, I don't know what your name is, but I know you's a white man. I'm a nigger, but I got a name jus' like you have. My name's Webb. If you call Webb, I'll come jus' as quick as I will for any other name and a lot more willing. If you don't want to say Webb, you can jus' say "Let's go," and you'll find me right there.' He looked at me a moment, and then he said, 'Where you from?' I said, 'I'm from Georgia, but I came on this boat from Little Hock.' He put his arm around my shoulder and said, 'Come on upstairs.' We had two or three drinks upstairs, and he said, 'You and your pardner are the only two men I have that is worth a damn.' Then he said, 'But you are right; you have a name, and you have a right to be called by it.' And from then on, he quit callin' us out of our names.

"But I only stayed on the boat six months. It wasn't because of the captain. Them niggers was bad. They gambled all the time, and I gambled with them. But they wouldn't stop at that. They would argue and fight and cut and shoot. A man would shoot a man down, and then kick him off into the river. Then when there was roll call, nobody would know what became of him. I didn't like that. I knew that I was goin' to kill somebody if I stayed on that boat 'cause I didn't intend for nobody to kill me. So I stopped.

"After that, I went back to the man that I worked for the month for and stayed with him till I married. I took care of the stock. I was only married once. My wife died the fourteenth of October. We had three children, and I have one daughter living.

"I have voted often. I never had no trouble. I am a colored man and I ain't got nothin' but my character, but I take care of that. I let them know I am in Arkansas. I ain't been out of Arkansas but to Memphis and Vicksburg, and I took them trips on the boat I was working on. I was a good man then.

"I can't say nothing about these wild-headed young people. They ain't got no sense. Take God to handle them.

"Some parts of politics are all right and some are all wrong. It is like Grant. He was straddled the fence part of the time. I believe Roosevelt wants eight more years. Of course, he did a great deal for the people but the working man isn't getting enough money. Prices are so high and wages so low that a man keeps up to the grindstone and never gets ahead. They don't mean for a colored man to prosper by money. Senator Robinson said a nigger wasn't worth but fifty cents a day. But the nigger is coming anyhow. He is stinching hisself and doing without. The young folks ain't doing it though. These young folks doing every devilishmcnt on earth they can. Look at that boy they caught the other day who had robbed twenty houses. This young race ain't goin' to stan' what I stood for. They goin' to school every day but they ain't learning nothin'. What will take us through this tedious journey through the world is his manners, his principle, and his behavior. Money ain't goin' to do it. You can't get by without principles, manner, and good behavior. Niggers can't do it. And white folks can't either."

---

**Pine Bluff District**
**FOLKLORE SUBJECTS**
**Name of Interviewer: Martin - Barker**
**Subject: (Negro Lore)--Ex-Slave**
**Story:—Information**

**This information given by: Alfred Wells**
**Place of Residence:**
**Occupation:**
**Age: 77**

[TR: Information moved from bottom of first page.]

I has de eye of an eagle. One in my haid, de other in my chest. Sometimes us slaves would stay out later at night than ole marster seid we could and they send the patrols out for us.

And we started a song; "Run nigger run, the petlo' catch you, run nigger run, its almost day."

My brother run off and hid in the pasture. I wuz a small boy, dey called me nigger cowboy, cause I drive de cows up at night, and took em to de paster in the mornings.

I knowed my brother runned off, but I wouldn't tell on him. He run off to join the Yankees. They never found him, although, they used the nigger dogs, who were taken out by men who were looking for runaway nigger slaves.

Ef I had my choice, I'd ruther be a slave. But we cant always have our ruthers. Them times I had good food, plenty to wear, and no more work than was good for me.

Now I is kinder miliated, when I think of what a high stepper I used to be. Having, to hang around with a sack on my back begging de government to keep me fum starving.

---

**Interviewer: Mrs. Bernice Bowden**
**Person interviewed: Douglas Wells**
**1419 Alabama Street, Pine Bluff, Arkansas**
**Age: 83**

"I'se just a kid 'bout six or seven when the war started and 'bout ten or twelve when it ceasted.

"I'se born in Mississippi on Miss Nancy Davis' plantation. Old Jeff Davis was some relation.

"My brother Jeff jined the Yankees but I never seen none till peace was declared.

"I heered the old folks talkin' and they said they was fightin' to keep the people slaves.

"I 'member old mistress, Miss Nancy. She was old when I was a kid. She had a big, large plantation. She had a lot of hands and big quarter houses. Oh, I 'member you could go three miles this way and three miles that way. Oh, she had a big plantation. I reckon it was mighty near big as this town. I 'member they

81

used to take the cotton and hide it in the woods. I guess it was to keep the Yankees from gettin' it.

"I lived in the quarters with my father and mother and we stayed there after the war—long time after the war. I stayed there till I got to be grown. I continued there. I 'member her house and yard. Had a big yard.

"I can read some. Learned it at Miss Nancy Davis' plantation after the war. They had a little place where they had school. I went to church some a long time ago.

"Abraham Lincoln was a white man. He fought in the time of the war, didn't he? Oh, yes, he issued freedom. The Yankees and the Rebels fought.

"After the war I worked at farm work. I ain't did no real hard work for over a year."

**Interviewer: Miss Irene Robertson**
**Person interviewed: John Wells, Edmondson, Arkansas**
**Age: 82**

"I was born down here at Edmondson, Arkansas. My owner was a captain in the Rebel War (Civil War). He run us off to Texas close to Greenville. He was keeping us from the Yankees. In fact my father had planned to go to the Yankees. My mother died on the way to Texas close to the Arkansas line. She was confined and the child died too. We went in a wagon. Uncle Tom and his wife and Uncle Granville went too. He left his wife. She lived on another white man's farm. My master was Captain R. Campbell Jones. He took us to Texas. He and my father come back in the same wagon we went to Texas in. My father (Joe Jones Wells) told Captain R. Campbell Jones if he didn't let him come back here that he would be here when he got here—beat him back. That's what he told him. Captain brought him on back with him.

"What didn't we do in Texas? Hooeee! I had five hundred head of sheep belonging to J. Gardner, a Texan, to herd every day—twice a day. Carry 'em off in the morning early and watch 'em and fetch 'em back b'fore dark. I was a shepherd boy is right. I liked the job till the snow cracked my feet open. No, I didn't have no shoes. Little round cactuses stuck in my feet.

"I had shoes to wear home. Captain Jones gave leather and everything needed to Uncle Granville. He was a shoemaker. He made us all shoes jus' before we was to start back. Captain Jones sent the wagon back for us. My father come back right here at Edmondson and farmed cotton and corn. Uncle Tom and Uncle Granville raised wheat out in Texas. They didn't have no overseer but they said they worked harder 'an ever they done in their lives, 'fore or since.

"My father went to war with his master. Captain Jones served 'bout three years I judge. My father went as his waiter. He got enough of war, he said.

"Captain R. Campbell Jones had a wife, Miss Anne, and no children. I seen mighty near enough war in Texas. They fit there. Yes ma'am, they did. I seen soldiers in Greenville, Texas. I seen the cavalry there. They looked so fine. Prettiest horses I ever seen.

"Freedom! Master Campbell Jones come to us and said, 'You free this morning. The war is over.' It been over then but travel was slow. 'You all can go back home, I'll take you, or you can go root hog or die.' We all got to gatherin' up our belongings to come back home. Tired of no wood neither, besides that hard work. We all share cropped with Captain R. Campbell Jones two years. I know that. We got plenty wood without going five or six miles like in Texas. After freedom folks got to changing 'bout to do better I reckon. I been farmin' right here all my life. We didn't have a lot to eat out in Texas neither. Mother was a farm woman too.

"I never seen a Ku Klux. Bad Ku Klux sound sorter like good Santa Claus. I heard 'em say it was real. I never seen neither one.

"I did own ten acres of land. I own a home now.

"My father drove a grub wagon from Memphis to Lost Swamp Bottom—near Edmondson—when they built this railroad through here.

"Father never voted. I have voted several times.

"Present times is tougher now than before it come on. Things not going like it ought somehow. We wants more pension. Us old folks needs a good living 'cause we ain't got much more time down here.

"Present generation—they are slack—I means they slack on their parents, don't see after them. They can get farm work to do. They waste their money more than they ought. Some folks purty nigh hungry. That is for a fact the way it is going.


### Edmondson, Arkansas

"Master Henry Edmondson owned all the land to the Chatfield place to Lehi, Arkansas. He owned four or five thousand acres of land. It was bottoms and not cleared. They had floods then, rode around in boats sometimes. Colored folks could get land through Andy Flemming (colored man). Mr. Henry Edmondson and whole family died with the yellow fever. He had several children—Miss Emma, Henry, and Will I knowed. It is probably his father buried at far side of this town. A rattlesnake bit him. Lake Rest or Scantlin was a boat landing and that was where the nearest white folks lived to the Edmondsons. I worked for Mr. Henry Edmondson, the one died with yellow fever. He was easy to work for. Land wasn't cleared out much. He was here before the Civil War. Good many people, in fact all over there, died of yellow fever at Indian Mound. Me and my brother waited on white folks all through that yellow fever plague. Very few colored folks had it. None of 'em I heered tell of died with it. White folks died in piles. Now when the smallpox raged the colored folks had it seem like heap more and harder than white folks. Smallpox used to rage every few years. It break out and spread. That is the way so many colored folks come to own land and why it was named Edmondson. Named for Master Henry—Edmondson, Arkansas.

"Mrs. Cynthia Ann Earle wrote a diary during the Civil War. It was partly published in the Crittenden County Times—West Memphis paper—Fridays, November 27 and December 4, 1936. She tells interesting things happening. Mentions two books she is reading. She tells about a flood, etc. She tells about visiting and spending over a thousand dollars. Mrs. L.A. Stewart or Mrs. H.E. Weaver of Edmondson owns copies if they cannot be obtained at the printing office at West Memphis."

**Interviewer: Samuel S. Taylor**
**Person interviewed: Sarah Wells**
**1012 W. Sixteenth Street, Little Rock, Arkansas**
**Age: 84**
**Occupation: Field hand**

"I was born in Warren County, Mississippi, on Ben Watkins' plantation. That was my master—Ben Worthington. I don't know nothin' about the year but it was before the war—the Civil War. I was born on Christmas day.

"Isaac Irby was my father. I don't know how you spell it. I can't read and write. I can tell you this. My mother's dead. She's been dead since I was twelve years old. Her name was Jane Irby. My name is Wells because I have been married. Willis was my husband's name. I have just been married once. I was married to him fifty years. He has been dead thirteen years the fifteenth of October. I don't know how old I was when I was married. But I know I am eighty-four years old now. I must have been about twenty or twenty-one when I married.

## Slave Houses

"The slaves lived in log houses, dirt chimneys, plank floors. They had beds made out of wood—that's all I know. I don't know where they kept their food. They kept it in the house when they had any. The slaves didn't have to cook much. Mars Ben had a slave to cook for them. They all et breakfast together, and lunch in the fiel'.

## Food and Cooking

"There was a great big shed. They'd all go up there and eat—the slaves would all go up and eat. I don't know what the grown folks had. They used to give us children milk and corn bread for breakfast. They'd give us greens, peas, and all like that for dinner. Didn't know nothin' about no lunch.

## Work and Runaways; Day's Work

"My mother and father worked in the field hoeing, plowing and all like that—doing whatever they told 'em to do. They raised corn and ground meal. Some of the slaves would pick five hundred pounds of cotton in a day; some of them would pick three hundred pounds; and some of them only picked a hundred. IF YOU DIDN'T PICK TWO HUNDRED FIFTY POUNDS, THEY'D PUNISH YOU, put you in the stocks. If you'd run off, they put the nigger hounds behind you. I never run off, but my mother run off.

"She would go in the woods. I don't know where she'd go after she'd get in the woods. She would go in the woods and hide somewheres. She'd take somethin' to eat with her. I couldn't find her myself. She take somethin' to eat with her. She didn't know what flour bread was. I don't remember what she'd take—somethin' she could carry. Sometimes she would stay in the woods two months, sometimes three months. They'd pay for the nigger hounds and let them chase her back. She'd try to get away. She never took me with her when she ran away.

## Buying and Selling

"My mother and her sister were bought in old Virginny. Ben Watkins was the one that bought her. He bought my father too. Then he sold my father to the Leightons. Leighton bought my father from Ben Watkins for a carriage driver. I was never bought nor sold. I was born on Ben Watkins' plantation and freed on it.

## Patrollers

"I've heered them say the pateroles is out. I don't know who they was. I know they'd whip you. I was a child then. I would just know what I was told mostly.

### How Freedom Came

"The Yankees told my mother she was free. They had on blue clothes. They said them was the Yankees. I don't know what they told her. I know they said she was free. That's all I know.

"Sometimes the soldiers would do right smart damage. They set a lot of houses on fire. They done right smart damage.

### Jeff Davis

"I have seen Jeff Davis. I never seen Lincoln. They said it was Jeff Davis I seen. I seen him in Vicksburg. That was after the war was over.

### Ku Klux Klan

"I have heered about the Ku Klux, but I don't know what it was I heered. They never bothered me.

### Right after the War

"Right after the war, my mother and father hired out to work. They did most any kind of work—whatever they could get to do. Mother cooked. Father would generally do house cleaning. Mother didn't live long after the war.

## Blood Poisoning

"I lost my finger because of blood poisoning. I had a scratch on my finger. Pulled a hangnail out of it. I went around a lady who had a high fever and she asked me to sponge her off and I did it. I got the finger in the water that I sponged with and it got blood poisoned. I like to have died.

## Father's Death

"I was married and had three children when my father died. I don't know what he died with nor what year.

"My mother had had seven children—all girls. I had seven children. But three of mine were boys and four were girls. Ain't none of them living now.

## Little Rock

"My son was living in Little Rock and he kept after me to come here and I come. After I come, he left and went to Kansas City. He died there. I used to do laundry work. I quit that. I commenced to do sellin' for different companies. I sold for Mack Brady, Crawford & Reeves, and a lot of 'em.

## Opinions

"I don't know what I think about the young people. They ain't nothin' like I was when I was a gal. Things have changed since I come along. I better not say what I think."

## Interviewer's Comment

The interviewee says she is eighty-four, and her story hangs together. Her husband died thirteen years ago, and they had been married fifty years when he died. She "recollects" being about twenty years old when she married. She says she was about twelve years old when her mother died, one year after the close of the Civil War. This data seems to be rather conclusive on the age of eighty-four.

---

**Interviewer: Miss Irene Robertson**
**Person interviewed: Sarah Williams Wells, Biscoe, Arkansas**
**Age: Born 1866**

"I jess can't tell much; my memory fails me. My white folks was John and Mary Williams but I was born two years after the surrender. Soon after the surrender they went to Lebanon, Tennessee. My folks stayed on wha I was born round in Murry County. My father was killed after the war but I was little. My mother died same year I married. I heard em say there was John and Frank. They may be living over there now. I heard em talking bout war times. They said my father was a blacksmith in the war. I come here wid four little children on a ticket to Crocketts Bluff. We was sick all that year. Made a fine crop. The man let another man have us to work. He was a colored man. His wife she was mean to us. She never come to see or do one thing when we all had fever. The babies nearly starved. Took all for doctor bills and medicine. Had $12 when all bills settled out of the whole crop. In all I had fifteen children. But two girls and one boy all that livin now. I farmed and washed and ironed all my life. My husband was born a slave. (He recently died.)

"The present generation ain't got no religion. They dances and cuts up a heap. They don't care nothing bout settlin down. When they marry now, that man say he got the law on her. She belongs to him. He thinks he can make her do like he wants her all the time and they don't get along. Now that's what I hear round. I sho got married and we got along good till he died. We treated one another best we knowed how. The times is what the folks making it. Time ain't no different, is like the folks make. This depression is whut the folks is making. Some so scared they won't get it all. They leave mighty little for the rest to get. They ain't nothin matter with nothin but the greedy people want it all to split through wid. I don't know what going to come of it all. Nothin I tell you bout it ain't no good. Young folks done smarter than I is. They don't listen to nobody."

**Interviewer: Miss Irene Robertson**
**Person interviewed: John Wesley, Helena, Arkansas**
**Age: ?**

"I was full grown when the Civil War come on. I was a slave till 'mancipation. I was born close to Lexington, Kentucky. My master in Kentucky was Master Griter. He was 'fraid er freedom. Father belong to Averys in Tennessee. He was a farm hand. They wouldn't sell him. I was sold to Master Boone close to Moscow. I was sold on a scaffold high as that door (twelve feet). I seen a lot of children sold on that scaffold. I fell in the hands of George Coggrith. We come to Helena in wagons. We crossed the river out from Memphis to Hopefield. I lived at Wittsburg, Arkansas during the war. They smuggled us about from the Yankees and took us to Texas. Before the war come on we had to fight the Indians back. They tried to sell us in Texas. George Coggrith's wife died. Mother was the cook for all the hands and the white folks too. She raised two boys and three girls for him. She went on raising his children during the war and after the war. During the war we hid out and raised cotton and corn. We hid in the woods. The Yankees couldn't make much out in the woods and canebrakes. We stayed in Texas about a year. Four years after freedom we didn't know we was free. We was on his farm up at Wittsburg. That is near Madison, Arkansas. Mother wouldn't let the children get far off from our house. She was afraid the Indians would steal the children. They stole children or I heard they did. The wild animals and snakes was one thing we had to look out for. Grown folks and children all kept around home unless you had business and went on a trip.

"My wife died three years ago. I stay with a grandchild. I got a boy but I don't know where he is now.

"I had a acre and a home. I got in debt and they took my place.

"I voted. The last time for President Wilson. We got a good President now. I voted both kinds of tickets some. I think they called me a Democrat. I quit voting. I'm too old.

"I farmed in my young days. I oil milled. I saw milled. I still black smithing (in Helena now). I make one or two dollars a week. Work is hard to git. Times is tight. I don't get help 'ceptin' some friend bring us some work. I stay up here all time nearly.

"I don't know about the young generation.

"Well, we had a gin. During of the war it got burnt and lots of bales of cotton went 'long with it.

"The Ku Klux come about and drink water. They wanted folks to stay at home and work. That what they said. We done that. We didn't know we was free nohow. We wasn't scared."

---

**Interviewer: Miss Irene Robertson**
**Person interviewed: Robert Wesley, Holly Grove, Arkansas**
**Age: 74**

"I was born in Shelby County, Alabama. My parents was Mary and Thomas Wesley. Their master was Mary and John Watts.

"John Watts tried to keep me. I stayed round him all time and rode up behind him on his horse. He was a soldier.

"Both my parents was sold but I don't know how it was done. There was thirteen children in our family. The white folks had a picnic and took colored long to do round. Some heard bout freedom and went home tellin' bout it. We stayed on and worked.

"The Ku Klux sure did run some of em. Seem like they didn't know what freedom meant. Some of em run off and kept goin'. Never did get back. I don't know a thing bout the Ku Klux. I heard em say they got whoopin's for doin' too much visitin'. I was a baby so I don't know.

"I do not vote. I voted for McKinley in Mississippi.

"I been farmin' all my life. I got one hog and a garden, three little grand babies. My daughter died and their papa went off and left em. Course I took em—had to. I pay $1 house rent. I get $12 from the PWA.

"The times is mighty fast. I recken the young folks do fair. There has been big changes since I come on."

---

**Interviewer: Miss Irene Robertson**
**Person interviewed: Maggie Wesmoland, Brinkley, Arkansas**
**Age: 85**

"I was born in Arkansas in slavery time beyond Des Arc. My parents was sold in Mississippi. They was brought to Arkansas. I never seed my father after the closing of the war. He had been refugeed to Texas and come back here, then he went on back to Mississippi. Mama had seventeen children. She had six by my stepfather. When my stepfather was mustered out at De Valls Bluff he come to Miss (Mrs.) Holland's and got mama and took her on wid him. I was give to Miss Holland's daughter. She married a Cargo. The Hollands raised me and my sister. I never seen mama after she left. My mother was Jane Holland and my father was Smith Woodson. They lived on different places here in Arkansas. I had a hard time. I was awfully abused by the old man that married Miss Betty. She was my young mistress. He was poor and hated Negroes. He said they didn't have no feeling. He drunk all the time. He never had been used to Negroes and he didn't like em. He was a middle age man but Miss Betty Holland was in her teens.

"No, mama didn't have as hard a time as I had. She was Miss Holland's cook and wash woman. Miss Betty told her old husband, 'Papa don't beat his Negroes. He is good to his Negroes.' He worked overseers in the field. Nothing Miss Betty ever told him done a bit of good. He didn't have no feeling. I had to go in a trot all the time. I was scared to death of him—he beat me so. I'm scarred up all over now where he lashed me. He would strip me start naked and tie my hands crossed and whoop me till the blood ooze out and drip on the ground when I walked. The flies blowed me time and again. Miss Betty catch him gone, would grease my places and put turpentine on them to kill the places blowed. He kept a bundle of hickory switches at the house all the time. Miss Betty was good to me. She would cry and beg him to be good to me.

"One time the cow kicked over my milk. I was scared not to take some milk to the house, so I went to the spring and put some water in the milk. He was snooping round (spying) somewhere and seen me. He beat me nearly to death. I never did know what suit him and what wouldn't. Didn't nothing please him. He was a poor man, never been used to nothin' and took spite on me everything happened. They didn't have no children while I was there but he did have a boy before he died. He died fore I left Dardanelle. When Miss Betty Holland married Mr. Cargo she lived close to Dardanelle. That is where he was so mean to me. He lived in the deer and bear hunting country.

"He went to town to buy them some things for Christmas good while after freedom—a couple or three years. Two men come there deer hunting every year. One time he had beat me before them and on their way home they went to the Freemens bureau and told how he beat me and what he done it for—biggetness. He was a biggity acting and braggy talking old man. When he got to town they asked him if he wasn't hiding a little Negro girl, ask if he sent me to school. He come home. I slept on a bed made down at the foot of their bed. That night he told his wife what all he said and what all they ask him. He said he would kill whoever come there bothering about me. He been telling that about. He told Miss Betty they would fix me up and let me go stay a week at my sister's Christmas. He went back to town, bought me the first shoes I had had since they took me. They was brogan shoes. They put a pair of his sock on me. Miss Betty made the calico dress for me and made a body out of some of his pants legs and quilted the skirt part, bound it at the bottom with red flannel. She made my things nice—put my underskirt in a little frame and quilted it so it would be warm. Christmas day was a bright warm day. In the morning when Miss Betty dressed me up I was so proud. He started me off and told me how to go.

"I got to the big creek. I got down in the ditch—couldn't get across. I was running up and down it looking for a place to cross. A big old mill was upon the hill. I could see it. I seen three men coming, a white man with a gun and two Negro men on horses or mules. I heard one say, 'Yonder she is.' Another said, 'It don't look like her.' One said, 'Call her.' One said, 'Margaret.' I answered. They come to me and said, 'Go to the mill and cross on a foot log.' I went up there and crossed and got upon a stump behind my brother-in-law on his horse. I didn't know him. The white man was the man he was share croppin' with. They all lived in a big yard like close together. I hadn't seen my sister before in about four years. Mr. Cargo told me if I wasn't back at his house New Years day he would come after me on his horse and run me every step of the way home. It was nearly twenty-five miles. He said he would give me the worst whooping I ever got in my life. I was going back, scared not to be back. Had no other place to live.

"When New Year day come the white man locked me up in a room in his house and I stayed in there two days. They brought me plenty to eat. I slept in there with their children. Mr. Cargo never come after me till March. He didn't see me when he come. It started in raining and cold and the roads was bad. When he come in March I seen him. I knowed him. I lay down and covered up in leaves. They was deep. I had been in the woods getting sweet-gum when I seen him. He scared me. He never seen me. This white man bound me to his wife's friend for a year to keep Mr. Cargo from getting me back. The woman at the house and Mr. Cargo had war nearly about me. I missed my whoopings. I never got none that whole year. It was Mrs. Brown, twenty miles from Dardanelle, they bound me over to. I never got no more than the common run of Negro children but they wasn't mean to me.

"When I was at Cargo's, he wouldn't buy me shoes. Miss Betty would have but in them days the man was head of his house. Miss Betty made me moccasins to wear out in the snow—made them out of old rags and pieces of his pants. I had risings on my feet and my feet frostbite till they was solid sores. He would take his knife and stob my risings to see the matter pop way out. The ice cut my feet. He cut my foot on the side with a cowhide nearly to the bone. Miss Betty catch him outer sight would doctor my feet. Seem like she was scared of him. He wasn't none too good to her.

"He told his wife the Freemens Bureau said turn that Negro girl loose. She didn't want me to leave her. He despised nasty Negroes he said. One of them fellows what come for me had been to Cargo's and seen me. He was the Negro man come to show Patsy's husband and his share cropper where I was at. He whooped me twice before them deer hunters. They visited him every spring and fall hunting deer but they reported him to the Freemens Bureau. They knowed he was showing off. He overtook me on a horse one day four or five years after I left there. I was on my way from school. I was grown. He wanted me to come back live with them. Said Miss Betty wanted to see me so bad. I was so scared I lied to him and said yes to all he said. He wanted to come get me a certain day. I lied about where I lived. He went to the wrong place to get me I heard. I was afraid to meet him on the road. He died at Dardanelle before I come way from there.

"After I got grown I hired out cooking at $1.25 a week and then $1.50 a week. When I was a girl I ploughed some. I worked in the field a mighty little but I have done a mountain of washing and ironing in my life. I can't tell you to save my life what a hard time I had when I was growing up. My daughter is a blessing to me. She is so good to me.

"I never knowed nor seen the Ku Klux. The Bushwhackers was awful after the war. They went about stealing and they wouldn't work.

"Conditions is far better for young folks now than when I come on. They can get chances I couldn't get they could do. My daughter is tied down here with me. She could do washings and ironings if she could get them and do it here at home. I think she got one give over to her for awhile. The regular wash woman is sick. It is hard for me to get a living since I been sick. I get commodities. But the diet I am on it is hard to get it. The money is the trouble. I had two strokes and I been sick with high blood pressure three years. We own our house. Times is all right if

I was able to work and enjoy things. I don't get the Old Age Pension. I reckon because my daughter's husband has a job—I reckon that is it. I can't hardly buy milk, that is the main thing. The doctor told me to eat plenty milk.

"I never voted."

---

**Interviewer: Miss Irene Robertson**
**Person interviewed: Calvin West, Widener, Arkansas**
**Age: 68**

"Mother belong to Parson Renfro. He had a son named Jim Renfro. She was a cook and farm hand too. I never heard her speak much of her owners. Pa's owner was Dr. West and Miss Jensie West. He had a son Orz West and his daughter was Miss Lillie West. I never was around their owners. Some was dead before I come on. My pa was a cripple man. His leg was drawn around with rheumatism. During slavery he would load up a small cart wid cider and ginger cakes and go sell it out. He sold ginger cakes two for a nickel and I never heard how he sold the cider. I heard him tell close speriences he had with the patrollers. Some of the landowners didn't want him trespassing on their places. He got a part of the money he sold out for. I judge from what he said his owner got part for the wagon and horse. He sold some at stores before freedom. He farmed too. His name was Phillip West and mother's name was Lear West. He was a crack hand at making ginger cakes. He sold wagon loads in town on Saturday till he died. I was a boy nearly grown. They had ten children in all. I was born in Tate County, Mississippi.

"Mr. Miller had land here. I didn't work for him but he wanted me to come here and work his land. He give us tickets. He said this was new land and we could do better. We work a lot and make big crops and don't hardly get a living out of it. We come on the train here.

"We come in 1920. The way we got down here now it is bad. We make big crops and don't get much for it. We have no place to raise things to help out and pay big prices for everything. I work. But times is hard. That is the very reason it is hard. We got no place to raise nothing. (Hard road and ditch in front and cotton field all around it except a few feet of padded dirt and a wood pile.) Times is good and if a fellow could ever get a little ahead I believe he could stay ahead. Since my wife been sick we jes' can make it.

"We never called for no help. She cooked and I worked. She signed up but it will be a long time, they said, till they could get to her."

---

**Interviewer: Miss Irene Robertson**
**Person interviewed: Mary Mays West, Widener, Arkansas**
**Age: 65**

"My parents' names was Josie Vesey and Henry Mays. They had ten children and five lived to be full grown. I was born in Tate County, Mississippi. Mother died in childbirth when she was twenty-eight years old. I'm the mother of twelve and got five living. I been cooking out for white people since I was nine years old. I am a good cook they all tell me and I tries to be clean with my cooking.

"Mother died before I can remember much about her. My father said he had to work before day and all day and till after night in the spring and fall of the year. They ploughed with oxen and mules and horses all. He said how they would rest the teams and feed and still they would go on doing something else. They tromped cotton at night by torchlight. Tromped it in the wagons to get off to the gin early next morning.

"In the winter they built fences and houses and got up wood and cleared new ground. They made pots of lye hominy and lye soap the same day. They had a ashhopper set all time. In the summer is when they ditched if they had any of that to do. Farming has been pretty much the same since I was a child. I have worked in the field all my life. I cook in the morning and go to the field all evening.

"We just had a hard time this winter. I had a stroke in October and had to quit cooking. (Her eye is closed on her left side—ed.) I love farm life. The flood last year got us behind too. We could do fine if I had my health."

---

**Interviewer: Miss Irene Robertson**
**Person interviewed: Sylvester Wethington**
**Holly Grove, Arkansas**
**Age: 77**

"I recollect seeing the Malish (Malitia) pass up and down the road. I can tell you two things happened at our house. The Yankee soldiers come took all the stock we had all down to young mistress' mule. They come fer it. Young mistress got a gun, went out there, put her side saddle on the mule and climbed up. They let her an' that mule both be. Nother thing they had a wall built in betwix er room and let hams and all kinds provisions swing down in thor. It went unnoticed. I recken it muster been 3 ft. wide and long as the room. Had to go up in the loft from de front porch. The front porch wasn't ceiled but a place sawed out so you could get up in the loft. They used a ladder and went up there bout once a week. They swung hams and meal, flour and beef. They swung sacks er corn down in that place. That all the place where they could keep us a thing in de world to eat. They come an' got bout all we had. Look like starvation ceptin' what we had stored way."

**Interviewer: Miss Irene Robertson**
**Person interviewed: Joe Whitaker, Madison, Arkansas**
**Age: 70 plus**

"I'm a blacksmith; my pa was a fine blacksmith. He was a blacksmith in the old war (Civil War). He never got a pension. He said he loss his sheep skin. His owners was George and Bill Whitaker. Mother always said her owners was pretty good. I never heard my pa speak of them in that way. They was both born in Tennessee. She was never sold. I was born in Murray County, Tennessee too. My mother was named Fronie Whitaker and pa Ike Whitaker. Mother had eleven children. My wife is a full-blood Cherokee Indian. We have ten children and twenty-three grandchildren.

"I don't have a word to say against the times; they are close at present. Nor a word to say about the next generation. I think times is progressing and I think the people are advancing some too."

[TR: The following is typed, but scratched out by hand.]
**Interviewer's Comment**

Some say his wife is a small part African.

**Interviewer: Beulah Sherwood Hagg**
**Person interviewed: Mrs. Julia A. White, 3003 Cross St.,**
**Little Rock, Ark.**
**Age: 79**

Idiom and dialect are lacking in this recorded interview. Mrs. White's conversation was entirely free from either. On being questioned about this she explained that she was reared in a home where fairly correct English was used.

My cousin Emanuel Armstead could read and write, and he kept the records of our family. At one time he was a school director. Of course, that was back in the early days, soon after the war closed.

My father was named James Page Jackson because he was born on the old Jackson plantation in Lancaster county, Virginia. He named one of his daughters Lancaster for a middle name in memory of his old home. Clarice Lancaster Jackson was her full name. A man named Galloway bought my father and brought him to Arkansas. Some called him by the name of Galloway, but my father always had all his children keep the name Jackson. There were fourteen of us, but only ten lived to grow up. He belonged to Mr. Galloway at the time of my birth, but even at that, I did not take the name Galloway as it would seem like I should. My father was a good carpenter; he was a fine cook, too; learned that back in Virginia. I'll tell you something interesting. The first cook stove ever brought to this town was one my father had his master to bring. He was cook at the Anthony House. You know about that, don't you? It was the first real fine hotel in Little Rock. When father went there to be head cook, all they had to cook on was big fireplaces and the big old Dutch ovens. Father just kept on telling about the stoves they had in Virginia, and at last they sent and got him one; it had to come by boat and took a long time. My father was proud that he was the one who set the first table ever spread in the Anthony House.

You see, it was different with us, from lots of slave folks. Some masters hired their slaves out. I remember a drug store on the corner of Main and Markham; it was McAlmont's drug store. Once my father worked there; the money he earned, it went to Mr. Galloway, of course. He said it was to pay board for mother and us little children.

My mother came from a fine family,—the Beebe family. Angeline Beebe was her name. You've heard of the Beebe family, of course. Roswell Beebe at one time owned all the land that Little Rock now sets on. I was born in a log cabin where Fifth and Spring streets meet. The Jewish Synagogue is on the exact spot. Once we lived at Third and Cumberland, across from that old hundred-year-old-building where they say the legislature once met. What you call it? Yes, that's it; the Hinterlider building. It was there then, too. My father and mother had the kind of wedding they had for slaves, I guess. Yes, ma'am, they did call them "broom-stick weddings". I've heard tell of them. Yes, ma'am, the master and mistress, when they find a couple of young slave folks want to get married, they call them before themselves and have them confess they want to marry. Then they hold the broom, one at each end, and the young folks told to jump over. Sometimes they have a new cabin fixed all for them to start in. After Peace, a minister came and married my father and mother according to the law of the church and of the land.

The master's family was thoughtful in keeping our records in their own big family Bible. All the births and deaths of the children in my father's family was in their Bible. After Peace, father got a big Bible for our family, and—wait, I'll show you.... Here they are, all copied down just like out of old master's Bible.... Here's where my father and mother died, over on this page. Right here's my own children. This space is for me and my husband.

No ma'am, it don't make me tired to talk. But I need a little time to recall all the things you want to know 'bout. I was so little when freedom came I just can't remember. I'll tell you, directly.

I remember that the first thing my father did was to go down to a plantation where the bigger children was working, and bring them all home, to live together as one family. That was a plantation where my mother had been; a man name Moore—James Moore—owned it. I don't know whether he had bought my mother from Beebe or not. I can remember two things plain what happened there. I was little, but can still see them. One of my mother's babies died and Master went to Little Rock on a horse and carried back a little coffin under his arm. The mistress had brought mother a big washing. She was working under the cover of the wellhouse and tears was running down her face. When master came back, he said: "How come you are working today, Angeline, when your baby is dead?" She showed him the big pile of clothes she had to wash, as mistress said. He said: "There is plenty of help on this place what can wash. You come on in and sit by your little baby, and don't do no more work till after the funeral." He took up the little dead body and laid it in the coffin with his own hands. I'm telling you this for what happened later on.

A long time after peace, one evening mother heard a tapping at the door. When she went, there was her old master, James Moore. "Angeline," he said, "you remember me, don't you?" Course she did. Then he told her he was hungry and homeless. A man hiding out. The Yankees had taken everything he had. Mother took him in and fed him for two or three days till he was rested. The other thing clear to my memory is when my uncle Tom was sold. Another day when mother was washing at the wellhouse and I was playing around, two white men came with a big, broad-shouldered colored man between them. Mother put her arms around him and cried and kissed him goodbye. A long time after, I was watching one of my brothers walk down a path. I told mother that his shoulders and body look like that man she kissed and cried over. "Why honey," she says to me, "can you remember that?" Then she told me about my uncle Tom being sold away.

So you see, Miss, it's a good thing you are more interested in what I know since slave days. I'll go on now.

The first thing after freedom my mother kept boarders and done fine laundry work. She boarded officers of the colored Union soldiers; she washed for the officers' families at the Arsenal. Sometimes they come and ask her to cook them something special good to eat. Both my father and mother were fine cooks. That's when we lived at Third and Cumberland. I stayed home till I was sixteen and helped with the cooking and washing and ironing. I never worked in a cottonfield. The boys did. All us girls were reared about the house. We were trained to be lady's maids and houseworkers. I married when I was sixteen. That husband died four years later, and the next year I married this man, Joel Randolph White. Married him in March, 1879. In those days you could put a house on leased ground. Could lease it for five years at a time. My father put up a house on Tenth and Scott. Old man Haynie owned the land and let us live in the house for $25.00 a year until father's money was all gone; then we had to move out. The first home my father really owned was at 1220 Spring street, what is now. Course then, it was away out in the country. A white lawyer from the north—B.F. Rice was his name—got my brother Jimmie to work in his office. Jimmie had been in school most all his life and was right educated for colored boy then. Mr. Rice finally asked him how would he like to study law. So he did; but all the time he wanted to be a preacher. Mr. Rice tell Jimmie to go on studying law. It is a good education; it would help him to be a preacher. Mr. Rice tell my father he can own his own home by law. So he make out the papers and take care of everything so some persons can't take it away. All that time my family was working for Mr. Rice and finally got the home paid for, all but the last payment, and Mr. Rice said Jimmie's services was worth that. So we had a nice home all paid for at last. We lived there till father died in 1879, and about ten years more. Then sold it.

My father had more money than many ex-slaves because he did what the Union soldiers told him. They used to give him "greenbacks" money and tell him to take good care of it. You see, miss, Union money was not any good here. Everything was Confederate money. You couldn't pay for a dime's worth even with a five dollar bill of Union money then. The soldiers just keep on telling my father to take all the greenbacks he could get and hide away. There wasn't any need to hide it, nobody wanted it. Soldiers said just wait; someday the Confederate money wouldn't be any good and greenbacks would be all the money we had. So that's how my father got his money.

If you have time to listen, miss, I'd like to tell you about a wonderful thing a young doctor done for my folks. It was when the gun powder explosion wrecked my brother and sister. The soldiers at the Arsenal used to get powder in tins called canteens. When there was a little left—a tablespoon full or such like, they would give it to the little boys and show them how to pour it in the palm of their hand, touch a match to it and then blow. The burning powder would fly off their hand without burning. We were living in a double house at Eighth and Main then; another colored family in one side. They had lots of children, just like us. One canteen had a lot more powder in. My brother was afraid to pour it on his hand. He put a paper down on top of the stove and poured it out. It was a big explosion. My little sister was standing beside her brother and her scalp was plum blowed off and her face burnt terribly. His hand was all gone, and his face and neck and head burnt terribly, too. There was a young doctor live close by name Deuell. Father ran for him. He tell my mother if she will do just exactly what he say, their faces will come out fine. He told her to make up bread dough real sort of stiff. He made a mask of it. Cut holes for their eyes, nose holes and mouths, so you could feed them, you see. He told mother to leave that on till it got hard as a rock. Then still leave it on till it crack and come off by itself. Nobody what ever saw their faces would believe how bad they had been burnt. Only 'round the edges where the dough didn't cover was there any scars. Dr. Deuell only charged my father $50.00 apiece for that grand work on my sister and brother.

Yes ma'am, I'll tell you how I come to speak what you call good English. First place, my mother and father was brought up in families where they heard good speech. Slaves what lived in the family didn't talk like cottonfield hands. My parents sure did believe in education.

The first free schools in Little Rock were opened by the Union for colored children. They brought young white ladies for teachers. They had Sunday School in the churches on Sunday. In a few years they had colored teachers come. One is still living here in Little Rock. I wish you would go see her. She is 90 years old now. She founded the Wesley Chapel here. On her fiftieth anniversary my club presented her a gold medal and had "Mother Wesley" engraved on it. Her name is Charlotte E. Stevens. She has the first school report ever put out in Little Rock. It was in the class of 1869. Two of my sisters were graduated from Philander Smith College here in Little Rock and had post graduate work in Fisk University in Nashville, Tennessee. My brothers and sisters all did well in life. Allene married a minister and did missionary work. Cornelia was a teacher in Dallas, Texas. Mary was a caterer in Hot Springs. Clarice went to Colorado Springs, Colorado and was a nurse in a doctor's office. Jimmie was the preacher, as I told you. Gus learned the drug business and Willie got to be a painter. Our adopted sister, Molly, could do anything, nurse, teach, manage a hotel. Yes, our parents always insisted we had to go to school. It's been a help to me all my life. I'm the only one now living of all my brothers and sisters.

Well ma'am, about how we lived all since freedom; it's been good till these last years. After I married my present husband in 1879, he worked in the Missouri Pacific railroad shops. He was boiler maker's helper. They called it Iron Mountain shops then, though. 52 years, 6 months and 24 days he worked there. In 1922, on big strike, all men got laid off. When they went back, they had to go as new men. Don't you see what that done to my man? He was all ready for his pension. Yes ma'am, had worked his full time to be pensioned by the railroad. But we have never been able to get any retirement pension. He should have it. Urban League is trying to help him get it. He is out on account of disability and old age. He got his eye hurt pretty bad and had to be in the railroad hospital a long time. I have the doctor's papers on that. Then he had a bad fall what put him again in the hospital. That was in 1931. He has never really been discharged, but just can't get any compensation. He has put in his claim to the Railroad Retirement office in Washington. I'm hoping they get to it before he dies. We're both mighty old and feeble. He had a stroke in 1933, since he been off the railroad.

How we living now? It's mighty poorly, please believe that. In his good years we bought this little home, but taxes so high, road assessments and all make it more than we can keep up. My granddaughter lives with us. She teaches, but only has school about half a year. I was trying to educate her in the University of Wisconsin, but poor child had to quit. In summer we try to make a garden. Some of the neighbors take in washing and they give me ironing to do. Friends bring in fresh bread when they bake. It takes all my granddaughter makes to keep up the mortgage and pay all the rest. She don't have clothes decent to go.

I have about sold the last of the antiques. In old days the mistress used to give my mother the dishes left from broken sets, odd vases and such. I had some beautiful things, but one by one have sold them to antique dealers to get something to help out with. My church gives me a donation every fifth Sunday of a collection for benefit. Sometimes it is as much as $2.50 and that sure helps on the groceries. Today I bought four cents worth of beans and one cent worth of onions. I say you have to cut the garment according to the cloth. You ain't even living from hand to mouth, if the hand don't have something in it to put to the mouth.

No ma'am, we couldn't get on relief, account of this child teaching. One relief worker did come to see us. She was a case worker, she said. She took down all I told her about our needs and was about ready to go when she saw my seven hens in the yard. "Whose chickens out there?" she asked. "I keep a few hens," I told her. "Well," she hollered, "anybody that's able to keep chickens don't need to be on relief roll," and she gathered up her gloves and bag and left.

Yes ma'am, I filed for old age pension, too. It was in April, 1935 I filed. When a year passed without hearing, I took my husband down so they could see just how he is not able to work. They told me not to bring him any more. Said I would get $10.00 a month. Two years went, and I never got any. I went by myself then, and they said yes, yes, they have my name on file, but there is no money to pay. There must be millions comes in for sales tax. I don't know where it all goes. Of course the white folks get first consideration. Colored folks always has to bear the brunt. They just do, and that's all there is to it.

What do I think of the younger generation? I wouldn't speak for all. There are many types, just like older people. It has always been like that, though. If all young folks were like my granddaughter—I guess there is many, too. She does all the sewing, and gardening. She paints the house, makes the draperies and bed clothing. She can cook and do all our laundry work. She understands raising chickens for market but just don't have time for that. She is honest and clean in her life.

Yes ma'am, I did vote once, a long time ago. You see, I wasn't old enough at first, after freedom, when all the colored people could vote. Then, for many years, women in Arkansas couldn't vote, anyhow. I can remember when M.W. Gibbs was Police Judge and Asa Richards was a colored alderman. No ma'am! The voting law is not fair. It's most unfair! We colored folks have to pay just the same as the white. We pay our sales tax, street improvement, school tax, property tax, personal property tax, dog license, automobile license—they what have cars—; we pay utility tax. And we should be allowed to vote. I can tell you about three years ago a white lady come down here with her car on election day and ask my old husband would he vote how she told him if she carried him to the polls. He said yes and she carried him. When he got there they told him no colored was allowed to vote in that election. Poor old man, she didn't offer to get him home, but left him to stumble along best he could.

I'm glad if I been able to give you some help. You've been patient with an old woman. I can tell you that every word I have told you is true as the gospel.

---

STATE—Arkansas
NAME OF WORKER—Samuel S. Taylor
ADDRESS—Little Rock, Arkansas
DATE—December, 1938
SUBJECT—Ex-slave

[TR: Another interview with J. White, by a different interviewer.]
[TR: Repetitive information deleted from subsequent pages.]

## Circumstances of Interview

1. Name and address of informant—**Julia White**, 3003 Cross Street, Little Rock.

2. Date and time of interview—

3. Place of interview—3003 Cross Street, Little Rock, Arkansas

4. Name and address of person, if any, who put you in touch with informant—

5. Name and address of person, if any, accompanying you—

6. Description of room, house, surroundings, etc.—

## Personal History of informant

1. Ancestry—

2. Place and date of birth—Little Rock, Arkansas, 1858

3. Family—Two children

4. Places lived in, with dates—Little Rock all her life.

5. Education, with dates—

6. Occupations and accomplishments, with dates—

7. Special skills and interests—

8. Community and religious activities—

9. Description of informant—

10. Other points gained in interview—She tells of accomplishments made by the Negro race.


## Text of Interview (Unedited)

"I was born right here in Little Rock, Arkansas, eighty years ago on the corner of Fifth and Broadway. It was in a little log house. That used to be out in the woods. At least, that is where they told me I was born. I was there but I don't remember it. The first place I remember was a house on Third and Cumberland, the southwest corner. That was before the war.

"We were living there when peace was declared. You know, my father hired my mother's time from James Moore. He used to belong to Dick Galloway. I don't know how that was. But I know he put my mother in that house on Third and Cumberland while she was still a slave. And we smaller children stayed in the house with mother, and the larger children worked on James Moore's plantation.

"My father was at that time, I guess, you would call it, a porter at McAlmont's drug store. He was a slave at that time but he worked there. He was working there the day this place was taken. I'll never forget that. It was on September 10th. We were going across Third Street, and there was a Union woman told mamma to bring us over there, because the soldiers were about to attack the town and they were going to have a battle.

"I had on a pair of these brogans with brass plates on them, and they were flapping open and I tripped up just as the rebel soldiers were running by. One of

110

them said, "There's a like yeller nigger, les take her." Mrs. Farmer, the Union woman ran out and said, "No you won't; that's my nigger." And she took us in her house. And we stayed there while there was danger. Then my father came back from the drug store, she said she didn't see how he kept from being killed.

"At that time, there were about four houses to the block. On the place where we lived there was the big house, with many rooms, and then there was the barn and a lot of other buildings. My father rented that place and turned the outbuildings into little houses and allowed the freed slaves to live in them till they could find another place.

"My husband was an orphan child, and the people he was living with were George Phelps and Ann Phelps. They were freed slaves. That was after the war. They came here and had this little boy with them, that is how I come to meet that gentlemen over there and get acquainted with him. When they moved away from there Phelps was caretaker of the Oakland Cemetery. We married on the twenty-seventh day of March, 1879. I still have the marriage license. I married twice; my first husband was George W. Glenn and my maiden name was Jackson. I married the first time June 10, 1875. I had two children in my first marriage. Both of than are dead. Glenn died shortly after the birth of the last child, February 15, 1878.

"Mr. White is a mighty good man. He is put up with me all these years. And he took mighty good care of my children, them by my first husband as well as his own. When I was a little girl, he used to tell me that he wouldn't have me for a wife. After we were married, I used to say to him, 'You said you wouldn't have me, but I see you're mighty glad to get me.'

"I have the marriage license for my second marriage.

"There's quite a few of the old ones left. Have you seen Mrs. Gillam, and Mrs. Stephen, and Mrs. Weathers? Cora Weathers? Her name is Cora not Clora. She's about ninety years old. She's at least ninety years old. You say she says that she is seventy-four. That must be her insurance age. I guess she is seventy-four at that; she had to be seventy-four before she was ninety. When I was a girl, she was a grown woman. She was married when my husband went to school. That has been more than sixty years ago, because we've been married nearly sixty years. My sister Mary was ten years older than me, and Cora Weathers was right along with her. She knew my mother. When these people knew my mother they've been here, because she's been dead since '94 and she would have been 110 if she had lived.

"My mother used to feed the white prisoners—the Federal soldiers who were being held. They paid her and told her to keep the money because it was Union Money. You know at that time they were using Confederate money. My father kept it. He had a little box or chest of gold and silver money. Whenever he got any paper money, he would change it into gold or silver.

"Mother used to make these ginger cakes—they call 'em stage planks. My brother Jimmie would sell them. The men used to take pleasure in trying to cheat him. He was so clever they couldn't. They never did catch him napping.

"Somebody burnt our house; it was on a Sunday evening. They tried to say it caught from the chimney. We all like to uv burnt up.

"My father was a carpenter, whitewasher, anything. He was a common laborer. We didn't have contractors then like we do now. Mother worked out in service too. Jimmie was the oldest boy. He taught school too.

"My father set the first table that was ever set in the Anthony Hotel, he was the cause of the first stove being brought here to cook on.

"Some of the children of the people that raised my mother are still living. They are Beebes. Roswell Beebe was a little one. They had a colored man named Peter and he was teaching Roswell to ride and the pony ran away. Peter stepped out to stop him and Roswell said, 'Git out of the way Peter, and let Billie Button come'.

"I get some commodities from the welfare. But I don't get nothing like a pension. My husband worked at the Missouri Pacific shops for fifty-two years, and he don't git nothing neither. It was the Iron Mountain when he first went there on June 8, 1879. He was disabled in 1932 because of injuries received on the job in March, 1931. But they hurried him out of the hospital and never would give him anything. That Monday morning, they had had a loving cup given them for not having had accidents in the plant. And at three p.m., he was sent into the hospital. He had a fall that injured his head. They only kept him there for two days and two hours. He was hurt in the head. Dr. Elkins himself came after him and let him set around in the tool room. He stayed there till he couldn't do nothing at all.

"In 1881, he got his eye hurt on the job in the service of the Missouri Pacific. It was the Iron Mountain then. He was off about three or four months. They didn't pay his wages while he was off. They told him they would give him a lifetime job, but they didn't. His eye gave him trouble for the balance of his life. Sometimes it is worse than others. He had to go to the St. Louis Hospital quite often for about three or four years.

"When the house on Third and Cumberland was burnt, he rebuilded it, and the owners charged him such rent he had to move. He rebuilt it for five hundred dollars and was to get pay in rent. The owners jumped the rent up to twenty-five dollars a month. That way it soon took up the five hundred dollars. Then we moved to Eighth and Main. My brother Jimmie was in an accident there.

"He was pouring powder on a fire from an old powder horn and the flames jumped up in the horn and exploded and crippled his hand and burnt his face. Dr. Duel, a right young doctor, said he could cure them if father would pay him fifty dollars a piece. My sister was burnt at the same time as my brother. He had them make a thin dough, and put it over their faces and he cut pieces out for their eyes, and nose, and mouth. They left that dough on their faces and chest till the dough got hard and peeled off by itself. It left the white skin. Gradually the face got back to itself and took its right color again, so you couldn't tell they had ever been burnt. The only medicine the doctor gave them was Epsom salts. Fifty dollars for each child. I used that remedy on a school boy once and cured him, but I didn't charge him nothing.

"I have a program which was given in 1874. They don't give programs like that now. People wouldn't listen that long. We each of us had two and three, and some of us had six and seven parts to learn. We learnt them and recited them and came back the next night to give a Christmas Eve program. You can make a copy of it if you want.

"A.C. Richmond is Mrs. Childress' brother. Anna George is Bee Daniels' mother (Bee Daniels is Mrs. Anthony, a colored public school teacher here). Corinne

Jordan is living on Gaines between Eighth and Ninth streets. She is about seventy-five years old now. She was about Mollie's age and I was about five years older than Molly. Mary Riley is C.C. Riley's sister. C.C. Riley is Haven Riley's father. C.C. is dead now. Haven Riley was a teacher, at Philander Smith, for a while. He's a stenographer now. August Jackson and J.W. Jackson are my brothers. W.O. Emory became one of our pastors at Wesley. John Bush, everybody's heard of him. He had the Mosaic temple and got a big fortune together before he died, but his children lost it all. Annie Richmond is Annie Childress, the wife of Professor E.C. Childress, the State Supervisor. Corinne Winfrey turned out to be John Bush's wife. Willie Lane married W.O. Emory. Scipio Jordan became the big man in the Tabernacle. H.H. Gilkey went to the post office. He married Lizzie Hull. She's living still too."

## Extra Comment

The marriage license which Mrs. White showed me, was issued March 27, 1879, by A.W. Worthen, County Clerk, per W.H.W. Booker to Julia Glen and J.R. White. It carries the name of Reverend W.H. Crawford who was the Pastor of Wesley Chapel Church at that time. The license was issued in Pulaski County.

GRAND ENTERTAINMENT AT WESLEY CHAPEL
Wednesday Evening, Dec'r. 23, 1874

PROGRAMME

Part I

Address by the General Manager    Mr. A.C. Richmond

Song--We Come Today        By the School

Prayer            Rev. William Henry Crawford

Declamation--My Mother's Bible    Miss Annie George

Dialogue--Three Little Graves    Miss M. Upshaw and
            Miss M.A. Scruggs

Dialogue--About Heaven      Miss Julia Jackson and
            Miss Alice Richardson

Declamation--Mud Pie        Miss Amelia Rose

Declamation--Ducklins and    Miss Goren Jordan
  Ducklins

Dialogue--The Beggar      Mr. H.H. Gilkey and
            Mr. W.A.M. Cypers

Declamation--Work While     Master Albert Pryor
  You Work

Dialogue--The Miser       Mr. C.C. Riley and
            Mr. Charles Hurtt, Jr.

Declamation--Pretty Pictures    Miss Cally Sanders

Declamation--Into the Sunshine  Miss Mollie Jackson

Song--Joy Bells         By the School

Dialogue--Sharp Shooting     Master Asa Richmond,
            Scipio Jordan,
            and Miss Laura A. Morgan

Declamation--What I Know     Master Morton Hurtt

Declamation--The Side to Look On  Miss Dora Frierson

Dialogue--The Tattler       Miss Mary Alexander,

Miss M.A. Scrugg,
Miss Mary Rose

Declamation--Little Clara     Miss Rebecca Ferguson

Dialogue--John Williams' Choice   Scipio Jordan, H.H. Gilkey
and Julia Jackson

Declamation--A Good Rule
Miss Lilly Pryor

Declamation--Complaint of the Poor
Miss Riley

Dialogue--The Examination
L.H. Haney, Jackson Crawford
and John Richmond

THE END.


Part II.

Dialogue--The Maniac

Miss Willie Lane, A.C. Richmond,
Rafe May, and Master A. Pryon

Dialogue--Father, Dear Father;
or The Fruits of Drunkenness

John E. Bush, W.A.M. Cypers,
Wm. Emery, Miss Coren Winfrey,
Miss Maggie Green, and others.

Dialogue--An Awakening

116

# ARKANSAS NARRATIVES

Miss Mollie Pryor and
   Miss Annie Richmond

Dialogue--Betsy and I are out

Alex. Scruggs and W.A.M. Cypers

Declamation--Lily of the Valley

Miss Mary Foster

Dialogue--Hasty Judgment

C.C. Riley, A.C. Richmond,
   Cypers and Haney

Declamation--The Little Shooter

Master August Jackson

Dialogue--Practical Lesson

Miss Julia Jackson, and August Jackson

Declamation--Bird and the Baby

Miss Julia Foster

Dialogue--Scenes in the Police Court

Richmond, Bush, and Emery

Ballad--Yankee Doodle Dandy

J.E. Bush

# ARKANSAS NARRATIVES

Part III

Dialogue--Colloquy in Church

Alice Richardson and Mollie

Declamation--Lucy Gray

Miss Alice Moore

Dialogue--Matrimony

Miss Willie Lane, M.A. Scruggs,
Mary Alexander, Mr. C.C. Riley

Dialogue--Traveler

Morton Hurtt and Scipio Jordan

Declamation--Truth in Parenthesis

Alice Moore.

| | |
|---|---|
| Dialogue--Forty Years Ago | Ales, Scruggs, and J.P. Winfrey |
| Declamation--The Last Footfall | Lizzie Hull |
| Declamation--Gone with a Handsomer Man than Me | John E. Bush, Miss Maggie Green, and H.G. Clay |
| Declamation--Golden Side | Annie Richmond |
| Declamation--The Union was saved by the Colored | Swan Jeffries |

# ARKANSAS NARRATIVES

Volunteers

Dialogue--Relief Aid Saving    Maggie Scruggs, Mary Ross,
  Society                  Lizzie Hull, Alice Moore,
                     Mary Alexander, Mollie Pryor,
                     Annie Fairchild, Lizzie Wind,
                     Julia Jackson, J.E. Bush,
                     J.W. Jackson

Song-Dutch Band    A.C. Richardson, Wm. Emery,
                     J.H. Haney, W.A.M. Cypers,
                     J.O. Alexander, J.E. Bush,
                     J.W. Jackson

Declamation--Number One    Alice Richardson

Declamation--What to Wear, and    Miss Coren Winfrey
  How to Wear It

Dialogue--A Desirable    J.E. Bush, J.W. Jackson,
                     A.C. Richmond

Dialogue-The Little Bill    Marion Henderson, J.E. Bush,
                     Miss Willie Lane, Miss Laura A.
                     Morgan, Asa Richmond, Jr.

Dialogue--Country Aunt's Visit    Henry Jackson, Misses Allice and
                     Julia Crawford, Maggie Howell,
                     Julia Jackson

Dialogue--Beauty and the Beast    Marion Henderson, Julia Jackson,
  (six Scenes)             Laura Morgan, Mary Scruggs,
                     Mary Ross, Coren Winfrey,
                     Willie Lane, Lizzie Wind,
                     Alice Crawford, J.E. Bush,
                     J.P. Winfrey

Dialogue--How not to Get          M.A. Scruggs and Mary Alexander
  and Answer

Declamation--The Incidents of    John Richmond
  Travel

## Interviewer's Comment

This program was given on one night, and the participants doubled right back the next night on another lengthy program celebrating Christmas Eve.

## Interview (continued)

"The Commissary was on the northeast corner of Third and Cumberland. They used to call it the government commissary building. It took up a whole half block. Mrs. Farmer, the white woman, was living in what you call the old Henderliter Place, the building on the northwest corner, during the War. She was a Union woman, and was the one that took us in when the Confederate soldiers were passing and wanted to take us to Texas with them.

"I was so small I didn't know much about things then. When peace was declared a preacher named Hugh Brady, a white man, came here and he had my mother and father to marry over again.

"Mrs. Stephens' father was one of the first school-teachers here for colored people. There were a lot of white people who came here from the North to teach. Peabody School used to be called the Union School. Mrs. Stephens has the first report of the school dated 1869. It gives the names of the directors and all. J.H. Benford was one of the Northern teachers. Anna Ware and Louise Coffman and Miss Henley were teachers too.

"Mrs. Stephens is the oldest colored teacher in Little Rock. The A-B-C children didn't want the old men to teach us. So they would teach 'Lottie'—she was only twelve years old then—and she would hear our lessons. Then at recess time, we would all get out and play together. She was my play mama. Her father, William Wallace Andrews, the first pastor of Wesley Chapel M.E. Church, was the head teacher and Mr. Gray was the other. They were teaching in Wesley Chapel Church. It was then on Eighth and Broadway. This was before Benford's time. It was just after peace had been declared. I don't know where Andrews come from nor how much learning he had. Most of the people then got their learning from white children. But I don't know where he got his.

"Wesley was his first church as far as I know. Before the War all the churches were in with the white people. After freedom, they drew out. Whether Wesley was his first church or not, he was Wesley's first pastor. I got a history of the church."

"They had a real Sunday-school in those days. My sister when she was a child about twelve years old said three hundred Bible verses at one time and received a book as a prize. The book was named 'A Wonderful Deliverance' and other Stories, printed by the American Tract Society, New York, 150 Nassau Street. My sister's name was Mollie Jackson."

---

**Interviewer: Miss Irene Robertson**
**Person interviewed: Lucy White, Marianna, Arkansas**
**Age: 74**

"I was born on Jim Banks' place close to Felton. His wife named Miss Puss. Mama and all of young master's niggers was brought from Mississippi. I reckon it was 'fore I was born. Old master name Mack Banks. I never heard mama say but they was good to my daddy. They had a great big place in Mississippi and a good big place over here.

"I recollect seeing the soldiers prance 'long the road. I thought they looked mighty pretty. Their caps and brass buttons and canteens shining in the sun. They rode the prettiest horses. One of 'em come in our house one day. He told Miss Puss he was goiner steal me. She say, 'Don't take her off.' He give me a bundle er bread and I run in the other room and crawled under the bed 'way back in the corner. It was dark up under there. I didn't eat the bread then but I et it after he left. It sure was good. I didn't recollect much but seeing them pass the road. I like to watch 'em. My parents was field folks. I worked in the field. I was raised to work. I keep my clothes clean. I washed 'em. I cooked and washed and ironed and done field work all. When I first recollect Marianna, Mr. Lon Tau and Mr. Free Landing (?) had stores here. Dr. Steven (Stephen?) and Dr. Nunnaly run a drug store here. There was a big road here. Folks started building houses here and there. They called the town Mary Ann fo' de longest time.

"Well, the white folks told 'am, 'You free.' My folks worked on fer about twenty years. They'd give 'em a little sompin outer dat crap. They worked all sorter ways—that's right—they sure did. They rented and share cropped together I reckon after the War ended.

"The Ku Klux never bothered us. I heard 'bout 'em other places.

"I never voted and I never do 'sepect to now. What I know 'bout votin'?

"Well, I tell you, these young folks is cautions. They don't think so but they is. Lazy, no'count, spends every cent they gits in their hands. Some works, some work hard. They drink and carouse about all night sometimes. No ma'am, I did not do no sich er way. I woulder been ashamed of myself. I would. Times what done run away wid us all now. I don't know what to look fer now but I know times changing all the time.

"I gets ten dollars and some little things to eat along. I say it do help out. I got rheumatism and big stiff j'ints (enlarged wrist and knuckles)."

---

**Interviewer: Bernice Bowden**
**Person interviewed: David Whiteman (c)**
**Age: 88**
**Home: 104 N. Kansas Street, Pine Bluff, Arkansas.**

"How de do lady. Oh yes, I was a pretty good sized boy when the war started. My old marster was sponsible Smith. My young marster was his son-in-law. I member 'bout the Yankees and the "Revels". I member when a great big troop of 'em went to war. Some of 'em was cryin' and some was laughin'. I tried to get young marster to let me go with him, but he wouldn't let me. Old marster was too old to go and his son dodged around and didn't go either. I member he caught hisself a wild mustang and tied hisself on it and rode off and they never did see him again.

"I know when they was fightin' we use to hear the balls when they was goin' over. I used to pick up many a ball.

"I wish my recollection was with me like it used to be." (At this point his wife spoke up and said "Seems like since he had the flu, his mind is kinda frazzled.")

"Yes'm, I member the Ku Klux. They used to have the colored folks dodgin' around tryin' to keep out of their way."

**Interviewer: Mrs. Bernice Bowden**
**Person interviewed: Dolly Whiteside (c)**
**Age: 81**
**Home: 103 Oregon Street, Pine Bluff, Ark.**

"I reckon I did live in slavery times—look at my hair.

"I been down sick—I been right low and they didn't speck me to live.

"Well, I'll tell you. I was old enough to know when they runned us to Texas so the Yankees couldn't overtaken us. We was in Texas when freedom come, I remember I was sittin on the fence when the soldiers in them blue uniforms with gold buttons come. He said, "I come to tell you you is free". I didn't know what it was all about but everybody was sayin' "Thank God". I thought it was the judgment day and I was lookin' for God. I said to myself, I'm goin' have some buttons like that some day.

"Colonel Williams was my marster. My mother was a nurse and took care of the colored folks when they was sick. I remember when people wasn't given nothin' but blue mass, calomel, castor oil and gruel, and every body was healthier than they is now.

"I'm the only one livin' that my mother birthed in this world. I was born here, but I been travelin', I been to Memphis and around.

"No mam, I don't remember nothin' else. I done tole you all I know."

---

Interviewer: Samuel S. Taylor
Person interviewed: J.W. Whitfield
3100 W. Seventeenth Street, Little Rock, Arkansas
Age: About 60
Occupation: Preacher

"My father's name was Luke Whitfield. He was sixty-three years old when he died in 1902. He was twenty-six years old when the Civil War ended. He was a slave. There were three other boys in the family besides him. No girls.

"His old mars' name was Bill Carraway. They lived at Nubian [HW: New Bern], North Carolina.

"My father said that his work in slavery time was blacksmithing. He had to fix the wagons and the plow too. He said that was his work during the Civil War too. He worked in the Confederate army too.

"I remember him saying how they whipped him when he ran off. The overseer got after him to whip him and he and one of his friends ran off. As they jumped over the fence to go into the woods the old mars hit my daddy with a cat-o-nine tails. You see, they took a strap of harness leather and cut it into four thongs and then they took another and cut it into five thongs, and they tied them together. When you got one blow you got nine and when you got five blows you got forty-five. As his old mars hit him, he said. 'I got him one, sir; it was a good one too, sir, and a go-boy.'[HW: ?] But it was nine.

"My father told me how they married in slavery times. They didn't count marriage like they do now. If one landowner had a girl and another wanted that girl for one of his men, they would give him her to wife. When a boy-child was born out of this marriage they would reserve him for breeding purposes if he was healthy and robust. But if he was puny and sickly they were not bothered about him. Many a time if the boy was desirable, he was put on the stump and auctioned off by the time he was thirteen years old. They called that putting him on the block. Different ones would come and bid for him and the highest bidder would get him.

"My father spoke of a pass. That was when they wanted to see the girls they would have to get a pass from the old mars. My father would speak to his mars and get a pass. If he didn't have a pass, the other mars would give him a whipping and sent him back. I told you about how they whipped them. They used to use those cat-o-nine tails on them when they didn't have a pass.

"They lived in a log cabin dobbed with dirt and their clothes were woven on a loom. They got the cotton, spun it on the spinning-wheel, wove it on the loom on rainy days. The women spun the thread and wove the cloth. For the boys from five to fifteen years old, they would make long shirts out of this cloth. The shirts had deep scallops in them. Then they would take the same cloth and dye it with indigo and make pants out of it. The boys never wore those pants in the field. No young fellow wore pants until he began to court.

"My mother was a girl that was sold in Lenoir County, near Kenston, [HW: Kinston?] North Carolina. My father met her in a place called Buford, [HW: Beaufort? Carteret Co.] North Carolina. My father was sold several times. The owner sold her to his owner and they jumped over a broomstick and were married. My daddy's mars bought my mother for him. Her name was Penny."

---

**Interviewer: Miss Irene Robertson**
**Person interviewed: Sarah Whitmore, Clarendon, Arkansas**
**Age: 100**

**Note:** The interviewer found this ex-slave in small quarters. The bed, the room and the Negro were filthy. A fire burned in an ironing bucket, mostly papers and trash for fuel. During the visit of the interviewer a white girl brought a tray with a measuring cup of coffee and two slices of bread with butter and fruit spread between. When asked where she got her dinner she said "The best way I can" meaning somebody might bring it to her. Her hands are too stiff and shaky to cook. Her eye sight is so bad she cannot clean her room. Two WPA county visitors, girls, bathe her at intervals.

"I was born between Jackson and Brandon. Sure I was born down in Mississippi. My mother's name they tole me was Rosie. She died when I was a baby. My father named Richard Chamber. They called him Dick. He was killed direckly after the war by a white man. He was a Rebel scout. The man named Hodge. I seed him. He shot my father. Them questions been called over to me so much I most forgot 'em. Well some jes' lack 'em. My father's master was Hal Chambers and his wife Virginia. Recken I do 'member the Ku Klux. They scared me to death. I go under the bed every time when I see them about. Then was when my father was killed. He went off with a crowd of white men. They said they was Rebel scouts. All I know I never seed him no more since that evening. They killed him across the line, not far from Mississippi. Chambers had two or three farms. I was on the village farm. I had one brother. Chambers sent him to the salt works and I never seed him no more. I was a orphant.

"Chambers make you work. I worked in the field. I come wid a crowd to Helena. I come on a boat. I been a midwife to black and white. I used to cook some. I am master hand at ironin'. I have no children as I knows of. I never born none. I help raise some. I come on a fine big steamboat wid a crowd of people. I married in Arkansas. My husband died ten or twelve years ago. I forgot which years it was. I been livin' in this bery house seben years.

"The Government give me $10 a month. I would wash dishes but I can't see 'bout gettin' 'round no more.

"Don't ax me 'bout the young niggers. They too fast fo me. If I see 'em they talkin' a passel of foolish talk. Whut I knows is times is hard wid me shows you born.

"You come back to see me. If you don't I wanter meet you all in heaben. By, by, by."

---

**Interviewer: Watt McKinney**
**Person interviewed: Dock Wilborn**
**A mile or so from Marvell, Arkansas**
**Age: 95**

Dock Wilborn was born a slave near Huntsville, Alabama on January 7, 1843, the property of Dan Wilborn who with his three brothers, Elias, Sam, and Ike, moved to Arkansas and settled near Marvell in Phillips County about 1855.

According to "Uncle Dock" the four Wilborn brothers each owning more than one hundred slaves acquired a large body of wild, undeveloped land, divided this acreage between them and immediately began to erect numerous log structures for housing themselves, their Negroes, and their stock, and to deaden the timber and clear the land preparatory to placing their crops the following season. The Wilborns arrived in Arkansas in the early fall of the year and for several months they camped, living in tents until such time that they were able to complete the erection of their residences. Good, substantial, well-constructed and warm cabins were built in which to house the slaves, much better buildings "Uncle Dock" says than those in which the average Negro sharecropper lives today on Southern cotton plantations. And these Negroes were given an abundance of the same wholesome food as that prepared for the master's family in the huge kettles and ovens of the one common kitchen presided over by a well-trained and competent cook and supervised by the wife of the master.

During the period of slavery the more apt and intelligent among those of the younger Negroes were singled out and given special training for those places in which their talents indicated they would be most useful in the life of the plantation. Girls were trained in housework, cooking, and in the care of children while boys were taught blacksmithing, carpentrying, and some were trained for personal servants around the home. Some were even taught to read and to write when it was thought that their later positions would require this learning.

According to "Uncle Dock" Wilborn, slaves were allowed to enjoy many pleasures and liberties thought by many in this day, especially by the descendants of these slaves, not to have been accorded them, were entirely free of any responsibility aside from the performance of their alloted labors and speaking from his own experience received kind and just treatment at the hands of their masters.

The will of the master was the law of the plantation and prompt punishment was administered for any violation of established rules and though a master was kind, he was of necessity invariably firm in the administration of his government and in the execution of his laws. Respect and obedience was steadfastly required and sternly demanded, while indolence and disrespect was neither tolerated or permitted.

In refutation to often repeated expressions and beliefs that slaves were cruelly treated, provided with insufficient food and apparel and subjected to inhuman punishment, it is pointed out by ex-slaves themselves that they were at that time very valuable property, worth on the market no less than from one thousand to fifteen hundred dollars each for a healthy, grown Negro and that it is unreasonable to suppose that these slaveowners did not properly safeguard their investments with the befitting care and attention such valuable property demanded or that these masters would by rule or action bring about any condition adversely effecting the health, efficiency or value of their slaves.

The spiritual and religious needs of the slaves received the attention of the same minister who attended the like needs of the master and his family, and services were often conducted on Sunday afternoons exclusively for them at which times the minister exhorted his congregation to live lives of righteousness and to be at all times obedient, respectful and dutiful servants in the cause of both their earthly and heavenly masters.

In the days of slavery, on occasion of the marriage of a couple in which the participants were members of slave-owning families, it was the custom for the father of each to provide the young couple with several Negroes, the number of course depending on the relative wealth or affluence of their respective families. It seems, however, that no less than six or eight grown slaves were given in most instances as well as a like number of children from two to four years of age. This provision on the part of the parents of the newly-wedded pair was for the purpose as "Uncle Dock" expressed it to give them a "start" of Negroes. The children were not considered of much value at such an age and the young master and his wife found themselves possessed with the responsibility attached to their proper care and rearing until such time as they reached the age at which they could perform some useful labor. These responsibilities were bravely accepted and such children received the best of care and attention, being it is said often kept in a room provided for than in the master's own house where their needs could be administered to under the watchful eye and supervision of their owners. The food given these young children according to informants consisted mainly of a sort of gruel composed of whole milk and bread made of whole wheat flour which was set before them in a kind of trough and from which they ate with great relish and grew rapidly.

Slaveowners, as a rule, arranged for their Negroes to have all needed pleasure and enjoyment, and in the late summer after cultivation of the crops was complete it was the custom for a number of them to give a large barbecue for their combined groups of slaves, at which huge quantities of beef and pork were served and the care-free hours given over to dancing and general merry-making. "Uncle Dock" recalls that his master, Dan Wilborn, who was a good-natured man of large stature, derived much pleasure in playing his "fiddle" and that often in the early summer evenings he would walk down to the slave quarters with his violin remarking that he would supply the music and that he wished to see his "niggers" dance, and dance they would for hours and as much to the master's own delight and amusement as to theirs.

Dock Wilborn's "pappy" Sam was in some respects disobedient, prompted mainly so it seems by his complete dislike for any form of labor and which Dan Wilborn due to their mutual affection appeared to tolerate for long periods or until such time that his patience was exhausted when he would then apply his lash to Sam a few times and often after these periodical punishments Sam would escape to the dense forests that surrounded the plantation where he would remain for days or until Wilborn would enlist the aid of Nat Turner and his hounds and chase the Negro to bay and return him to his home.

"Uncle Dock" Wilborn and his wife "Aunt Becky" are among the oldest citizens of Phillips County and have been married for sixty-seven years. Dan Wilborn performed their marriage ceremony. The only formality required in uniting them as man and wife was that each jump over a broom that had been placed on the floor between them. This old couple are the parents of four children, the eldest of whom is now sixty-three. They live alone in a small white-washed cabin only a mile or so from Marvell being supported only by a small pension they receive each month from the Social Security Board. They have a garden and a few chickens and a hog or two and are happy and content as they dip their snuff and recall those days long past during which they both contend that life was at its best, "Aunt Becky" is religious and a staunch believer, a long-time member of Mount Moriah Baptist Church while "Uncle Dock" who has never been affiliated with any religious organization is yet as he terms himself "a sinner man" and laughingly remarks that he is going to ride into Heaven on "Aunt Becky's" ticket to which comment she promptly replies that her ticket is good for only one passage and that if he hopes to get there he must arrange for one of his own.

---

**Interviewer: Miss Irene Robertson**
**Person interviewed: Bell Wilks, Holly Grove, Arkansas**
**Age: 80**

"I was raised in Pulaski, Tennessee, Giles County. The post office was at one end of the town, bout half mile was the church down at the other end. Yes'm, that way Pulaski looked when I lived there. My father's master was Peter or Jerry Garn—I don't know which. They brothers? Yes'm.

"My mother's master was John Wilks and Miss Betty. Mama's name was Callie Wilks and papa's name was Freeman. Mama had seven children. She was a field hand. She said all on their place could do nearly anything. They took turns cooking. Seems like it was a week about they took milkin', doin' house work, field work, and she said sometimes they sewed.

"Father told my mother one day he was going to the Yankees. She didn't want him to go much. He went. They mustered out drilling one day. He had to squat right smart. He saw some cattle in the distance looked like army way off. He fell dead. They said it was heart disease. They brought him home and some of dem stood close to him drillin' told her that was way it happened.

"The man what owned my mother was sorter of a Yankee hisself. We all stayed till he wound up the crop. He sold his place and went to Collyoka on the L. and N. Railway. He give us two and one-half bushels corn, three bushels wheat, and some meat at the very first of freedom. When it played out we went and he give us more long as he stayed there.

"When mama left she went to a new sorter mill town and cooked there till 1869. She carried me to a young woman to nurse for her what she nursed at Mostor Wilks befo freedom. I stayed wid her till 1876. I sure does remember dem dates. (laughed)

"Yes'm, I was nursin' for Dr. Rothrock when that Ku Klux scare was all bout. They coma to our house huntin' a boy. They didn't find him. I cover up my head when they come bout our house. Some folks they scared nearly to death. I bein' in a strange place don't know much bout what all I heard they done.

"I don't vote. I don't know who to vote for, let people vote know how.

"I get bout $8 and some commodities. It sure do help me out too. I tell you it sure do."

---

**Interviewer: Miss Irene Robertson**
**Person interviewed: Bell Williams, Forrest City, Arkansas**
**Age: 85**

"We was owned by Master Rucker. It seems I was about ten years old when the Civil War started. It seems like a dream to me now. Mother was a weaver. They said she was a fine weaver. She wove for all on the place and some special pieces of cloth for outsiders. She wove woolen cloth too. I don't know whether they paid for the extra weaving or not. People didn't look on money like they do now. They was free with one another about eating and visiting and work too when a man got behind with the work. The fields get gone in the grass. Sometimes they would be sick or it rained too much. The neighbor would send all his slaves to work till they caught up and never charge a cent. I don't hear about people doing that way now.

"My parents was named Clinton and Billy Bell. There was nine of us children.

"I never seen nobody sold. Mother was darker. Papa was light—half white. They didn't talk in front of children about things and I never did know. I've wondered.

"After freedom my folks stayed on at Master Rucker's. I got to be a midwife. I nursed and was a house girl after the war. Then the doctors got to sending for me to nurse and I got to be a midwife.

"My father was a good Bible scholar. He preached all around Murfreesboro, Tennessee. He was a Methodist. He died when he was seventy-seven years old. He had read the Bible through seventy-seven times--one time for every year old he was."

---

**Mrs. Mildred Thompson**
**Mrs. Carol Graham**
**El Dorado District**
**Federal Writers Project**
**Union County, Arkansas**

**Charley Williams**, Ex-slave. Mawnin' Missy. Yo say wha Aint Fanny Whoolah live? She live right down de road dar in dat fust house. Yas'm. Dat wha she live. Yo say whut mah name? Mah name is Charley. Yas'm, Charley Williams. Did ah live in slavery time? Yas'm sho' did. Mah marster wuz Dr. Reed Williams and he live at Kew London (SE part of Union County) or ah speck ah bettuh say near New London caise he live on de Mere-Saline Road, de way de soldiers went and come. Marster died befo' de Civil Wah. Does ah membah hit? Yas'm ah say ah does. Ah wuz bo'n in 1856. Mah ole mutha died befo' de wah too. Huh name wuz Charity. Mah young marster went tuh de wah an come back. He fit at Vicksburg an his name wuz Bennie Williams. But he daid now tho. Dere was a hep uv dem white William Chillun. Dere wuz Miss Narcissi an she am a livin now at Stong. Den dere's Mr. Charley. Ah wuz named fuh him. He am a livin now too. Den dere is Mr. Race Williams. He am a livin at Strong too. Dere wuz Miss Annie, Miss Martha Jane and Miss Madie. Dey is all daid. When young marster would come by home or any uv de udder soldiers us little niggers would steal de many balls (bullets or shot) fum dey saddul bags and play wid em. Ah nevah did see so many soldiers in mah life. Hit looked tuh me like dey wuz enough uv em to reach clear cross de United States. An ah nevah saw de like uv cows as they had. Dey wuz nuff uv em to rech clar to Camden.

Is ah evah been mahried and does ah have any chillun? Yes'm. Yas'm. Ah's been mahried three times. Me an mah fust wife had seven chillun. When we had six chillun me and mah wife moved tuh Kansas. We had only been der 23 days when mah wife birthed a chile and her an de chile both died. Dat left me wid Carey Dee, Lizzie, Arthur, Richmond, Ollie and Lillie to bring back home. Ah mahried agin an me an dat wife had one chile name Robert. Me an mah third wife has three: Joe Verna, Lula Mae an Johnnie B.

Is dey hents? Ah've hearn tell uv em but nevah have seed no hants. One uv mah friens whut lived on the Hommonds place at Hillsboro could see em. His name wuz Elliott. One time me an Elliott wuz drivin along an Elliott said: "Charley, somebody got hole uv mah horse!" Sho nuff dat horse led right off inter de woods an comminced to buckin so Elliott and his hoss both saw de haint but ah couldn' see hit. Yo know some people jes caint see em.

Yas'm right up dere is wha Aint Fannie live. Yas'm. Goodday Missy."

## FOLK CUSTOMS

We found Fannie Wheeler at home but not an ex-slave. She was making a bedspread of tobacco sacks.

"Yas'm chillun ah'm piecing mahsef a bedspraid from dese heah backy sacks. Yas'm dey sho does make er nice spraid. See dat'n on mah baid. Aint hit purty. Hit wuz made fum backy sacks. Don yo all think dat yaller bodah (border) set hit off purty? Ah'm aimin to bodah dis'n wid pink er blue.

What am dat up dar in dat picture frame? Why dat am plaits of har (hair). Hits uv mah kin and frien's. When we would move way off dey would cut off a plait and give hit tuh us tuh membah dem by. Mos' uv dem is daid now but ah still membahs dem and ah kin name evah plait now."

We were told that Sallie Sims was an old negress and went to see her she was not an ex-slave either but she told us an interesting little story about

## HAINTS and BODY MARKS

"No'm, ah'm purty ole but ah wuz bo'n aftuh surrender. Is ah evah seen a hant? Now ah nevah did but once and mah ma said dat wuz a hant. Ah wuz out in de woods waukin (walking) an ah saw sumpin dat looked lak a squirrel start up a tree and de fudder up hit got the bigger hit got an hit wuz big as a bear when hit got to de top and ma said dat hit was a haint. Dat is de only time ah evah seed one.

Now mah granchillun can all see hants and mah little great gran' chile too. An evah one uv dem wuz bo'n wid a veil ovah dey face. Now when a chile is bo'n wid a veil ovah his face—if de veil is lifted up de sho can see hants and see evah thing but if'n de veil is pulled down stid up bein lifted up de won't see em. After de veil is pulled down an taken off, wrap hit up in a tissue paper and put hit in de trunk and let hit stay dar till hit disappear and de chile won't nevah see hants. Mah grandaughter what lives up north in Missouri come down heah to visit mah son's fambly an me ah an brang huh li'l boy wid huh. Dat chile is bout seben years ole an dat chile could see hants all in de house an he wouldn' go tuh baid till his gran'pappy come home an went tuh baid wid him.

---

**Interviewer: Miss Irene Robertson**
**Person interviewed: Charlie Williams**
**Brassfield; Ark.**
**Age: 73**

"I was born four miles from Holly Springs, Mississippi. My parents was named Patsy and Tom Williams. They had twenty children. Nat Williams and Miss Carrie Williams owned them both. They had four children.

"At freedom he was nice as could be—wanted em to stay on with him and they did. He didn't whip em. They liked that in him. His wife was dead and he come out to Arkansas with us. He died at Lonoke—Mr. Tom Williams at Lonoke.

"I farmed nearly all my life. I worked on a steamboat on White River five or six years—*The Ralph.*

"I never saw a Ku Klux. Mr. Williams kept us well protected.

"My mother's mother couldn't talk plain. My mother talked tolerably plain. She was a 'Molly Glaspy' woman. My father had a loud heavy voice; you could hear him a long ways off.

"I have no home. I am a widower. I have no land. I get a small check and commodities.

"I vote. I haven't voted in a long time. I'm not educated to know how that would serve us best."

---

**Interviewer: Samuel S. Taylor**
**Person interviewed: Columbus Williams**
**Temporary: 2422 Howard Street, Little Rock, Arkansas**
**Permanent: Box 12, Route 2, Ouachita County, Stevens, Arkansas**
**Age: 98**

"I was born in Union County, Arkansas, in 1841, in Mount Holly.

"My mother was named Clora Tookes. My father's name is Jordan Tookes. Bishop Tookes is supposed to be a distant relative of ours. I don't know my mother and father's folks. My mother and father were both born in Georgia. They had eight children. All of them are dead now but me. I am the only one left.

"Old Ben Heard was my master. He come from Mississippi, and brought my mother and father with him. They were in Mississippi as well as in Georgia, but they were born in Georgia. Ben Heard was a right mean man. They was all mean 'long about then. Heard whipped his slaves a lot. Sometimes he would say they wouldn't obey. Sometimes he would say they sassed him. Sometimes he would say they wouldn't work. He would tie them and stake them out and whip them with a leather whip of some kind. He would put five hundred licks on them before he would quit. He would buy the whip he whipped them with out of the store. After he whipped them, they would put their rags on and go on about their business. There wouldn't be no such thing as medical attention. What did he care. He would whip the women the same as he would the men.

"Strip 'em to their waist and let their rags hang down from their hips and tie them down and lash them till the blood ran all down over their clothes. Yes sir, he'd whip the women the same as he would the men.

"Some of the slaves ran away, but they would catch them and bring them back, you know. Put the dogs after them. The dogs would just run them up and bay them just like a coon or 'possum. Sometimes the white people would make the dogs bite them. You see, when the dogs would run up on them, they would sometimes fight them, till the white people got there and then the white folks would make the dogs bite them and make them quit fighting the dogs.

"One man run off and stayed twelve months once. He come back then, and they didn't do nothin' to him. 'Fraid he'd run off again, I guess.

"We didn't have no church nor nothing. No Sunday-schools, no nothin'. Worked from Monday morning till Saturday night. On Sunday we didn't do nothin' but set right down there on that big plantation. Couldn't go nowhere. Wouldn't let us go nowhere without a pass. They had the paterollers out all the time. If they caught you out without a pass, they would give you twenty-five licks. If you outrun them and got home, on your master's plantation, you saved yourself the whipping.

"The black people never had no amusement. They would have an old fiddle— something like that. That was all the music I ever seen. Sometimes they would ring up and play 'round in the yard. I don't remember the games. Sing some kind of old reel song. I don't hardly remember the words of any of them songs.

"Wouldn't allow none of them to have no books nor read nor nothin'. Nothin' like that. They had corn huskin's in Mississippi and Georgia, but not in Arkansas. Didn't have no quiltin's. Women might quilt some at night. Didn't have nothin' to make no quilts out of.

"The very first work I did was to nurse babies. After that when I got a little bigger they carried me to the field—choppin' cotton. Then I went to picking cotton. Next thing—pullin' fodder. Then they took me from that and put me to plowin', clearin' land, splittin' rails. I believe that is about all I did. You worked from the time you could see till the time you couldn't see. You worked from before sunrise till after dark. When that horn blows, you better git out of that house, 'cause the overseer is comin' down the line, and he ain't comin' with nothin' in his hand.

"They weighed the rations out to the slaves. They would give you so many pounds of meat to each working person in the family. The children didn't count; they didn't git none. That would have to last till next Sunday. They would give them three pounds of meat to each workin' person, I think. They would give 'em a little meal too. That is all they'd give 'em. The slaves had to cook for theirselves after they come home from the field. They didn't get no flour nor no sugar nor no coffee, nothin' like that.

"They would give the babies a little milk and corn bread or a little molasses and bread when they didn't have the milk. Some old person who didn't have to go to the field would give them somethin' to eat so that they would be out of the way when the folks come out of the field.

"The slaves lived in old log houses—one room, one door, *one window*, one everything. There were *plenty windows* though. There were windows all [HW: ?] around the house. They had cracks that let in more air than the windows would. They had plank floors. Didn't have no furniture. The bed would have two legs and would have a hole bored in the side of the house where the side rail would run through and the two legs would be out from the wall. Didn't have no springs and they made out with anything they could git for a mattress. Master wouldn't furnish them nothin' of that kind.

"The jayhawkers were white folks. They didn't bother we all much. That was after the surrender. They go 'round here and there and git after white folks what they thought had some money and jerk them 'round. They were jus' common men and soldiers.

"I was not in the army in the War. I was right down here in Union County then. I don't know just when they freed me but it was after the War was over. The old white man call us up to the house and told us now we was free as he was; that if we wanted to stay with him it was all right, if we didn't and wanted to go away anywheres, we could have the privilege to do it.

"Marriage wasn't like now. You would court a woman and jus' go on and marry. No license, no nothing. Sometimes you would take up with a woman and go on with her. Didn't have no ceremony at all. I have heard of them stepping over a broom but I never saw it. Far as I saw there was no ceremony at all.

"When the slaves were freed they expected to get forty acres and a mule. I never did hear of anybody gettin' it.

"Right after the War, I worked on a farm with Ben Heard. I stayed with him about three years, then I moved off with some other white folks. I worked on shares. First I worked for half and he furnished a team. Then I worked on third and fourth and furnished my own team. I gave the owner a third of the corn and a fourth of the cotton and kept the rest. I kept that up several years. They cheated us out of our part. If they furnished anything, they would sure git it back. Had everything so high you know. I have farmed all my life. Farmed till I got so old I couldn't. I never did own my own farm. I just continued to rent.

"I never had any trouble about voting. I voted whenever I wanted to. I reckon it was about three years after the War when I began to vote.

"I never went to school. One of the white boys slipped and learned me a little about readin' in slave time. Right after freedom come, I was a grown man; so I had to work. I married about four or five years after the War. I was just married once. My wife is not living now. She's gone. She's been dead for about twelve years.

"I belong to the A.M.E. Church and my membership is in the New Home Church out in the country in Ouachita County."

---

**Interviewer: Samuel S. Taylor**
**Person interviewed: Frank Williams**
**County Hospital, ward eleven, Little Rock, Arkansas**
**Age: 100, or more**

"I'm a hundred years old. I know I'm a hundred. I know from where they told me. I don't know when I was born.

"I been took down and whipped many a time because I didn't do my work good. They took my pants down and whipped me just the same as if I'd been a dog. Sometimes they would whip the people from Saturday night till Monday morning.

"I run off with the Yankees. I was young then. I was in the Civil War. I don't know how long I stayed in the army. I ain't never been back home since. I wish I was. I wouldn't be in this condition if I was back home.

"Mississippi was my home. I come up here with the Yankees and I ain't never been back since. Laconia, Mississippi was the place I used to be down there. I been wanting to go home, but I couldn't git off. I want to git you to write there for me. I belong to the Baptist church. Write to the elders of the church. I belong to the Mission Baptist Church on the other side of Rock Creek here.

"They just lived in log houses in slave time.

"I want to go back home. They made me leave Laconia.

"Pateroles!! Oh, my God!!! I know 'nough 'bout them. Child, I've heard 'em holler, 'Run, nigger, run! The pateroles will catch you.'

"The jayhawkers would catch people and whip them.

"I would be back home yet if they hadn't made me come away.

"They didn't have no church in slavery time. They jus' had to hide around and worship God any way they could.

"I used to live in Laconia. I ain't been back there since the war. I want to go back to my folks."

## Interviewer's Comment

Frank Williams is like a man suffering from amnesia. He is the first old man that I have interviewed whose memory is so far gone. He remembers practically nothing. He can't tell you where he was born. He can't tell you where he lived before he came to Little Rock. Only when his associates mention some of the things he formerly told them can he remember that little of his past that he does state in any remote approach to detail.

There is a strong emotional set which relates to his slave time experiences. The emotion surges up in his mind at any mention of slave time matters. But only the emotion remains. The details are gone forever. Names, times, places, happenings are gone forever. He does not even recall the name of his father, the name of his mother, or the name of any of his relatives or masters, or old-time friends. No single definite thing rises above the horizon of his mind and defines itself clearly to him.

And always after every sentence he utters, there rises the old refrain: "I want to go back home. I wouldn't be in this condition if I was back home. I live in Laconia. They made me come away." And that is the substance of the story he remembers.

---

**Interviewer: Thomas Elmore Lucy**
**Person interviewed: Gus Williams, Russellville, Arkansas**
**Age: 80**

"Was you lookin' for me t'oder day? Sure, my name's Williams—Gus Williams—not Wilson. Dey gits me mixed up wid dat young guy, Wilson.

"Yes, I remembers you—sure—talks to yo' brother sometimes.

"I was born in Chatham County, Georgia—Savannah is de county seat. My marster's name was Jim Williams. Never seen my daddy cause de Yankees carried him away durin' de War, took him away to de North. Old marster was good to his slaves, I was told, but don't ricollect anything about em. Of course I was too young. Was born on Christmas day, 1857—but I don't see anything specially interestin' in bein' a Christmas present; never got me nothin', and never will.

"Was workin' on WPA—this big Tech. buildin'—but got laid off t'other day.

"My mamma brought us to Arkansas in 1885, but we stopped and lived for several years in Tennessee. Worked for twelve years out of Memphis on the old Anchor Line steamboats on de Mississippi, runnin' from St. Louis to N'Orleans. Plenty work in dem days.

"No, I ain't voted in a long time; can't afford to vote because I never have the dollar. No dollar—no vote. Depression done fixed my votin'.

"Jest me and my wife, but it takes pluggin' away to get along. We belongs to the C.M.E. Church since 1915. I was janitor at the West Ward School for seven years, and sure liked dat job.

142

"Don't ask me anything about dese boys and gals livin' today. Much difference in dem and de young folks livin' in my time as between me and you. No dependence to be put in em. My *estimony* is dat de black servants today workin' for de whites learns things from dem white girls dat dey never knowed before, and den goes home and does things dey never done before.

"Don't ricollect many of de old-time songs, but one was somep'n like—"Am I Born to Die?" And—oh, yes,—lots of times we sung 'Amazin' Grace, how sweet de soun' dat saves a *race* like me.'

"No suh, I ain't got no education—never had a chance to git one."

**NOTE:** The underscored words are actual quotations. "Estimony" for "opinion" was a characteristic in Gus' vocabulary; "race" for the original "wretch" in the song may have been a general error in some local congregations.

---

**Interviewer: Pernella M. Anderson**
**Person interviewed: Henrietta Williams**
**B. Avenue, El Dorado, Arkansas**
**Age: About 82**

"I am about 82 years old. I was born in Georgia down in the cotton patch. I did not know much about slavery, for I was raised in the white folks' house, and my old mistress called me her little nigger, and she didn't allow me to be whipped and drove around. I remember my old master whipped me one time and old mistress fussed with him so much he never did whip me any more.

"I never had to get out and do any real hard work until I was nearly grown. My mother did not have but one child. My father was sold from my mother when I was about two years old and he was carried to Texas and I did not see him any more until I was 35 years old. So my mother married again when she was set free. I didn't stay with my mother very much. She stayed off in a little log house with a dirt floor, and she cooked on the fireplace with a skillet and lid, and the house had one window with a shutter. She had to cut logs and roll them like a man and split rails and plow. I would sometimes ask old mistress to let me go out where my mother was working to see her plow and when I got to be a big girl about nine years she began learning me how to plow.

"I often told the niggers the white folks raised me. The niggers tell me, 'Yes, the white folks raise you but the niggers is going to kill you.'

"After freedom my mistress and master moved to Louisiana. They farmed. They owned a big plantation. I did the housework.

"The biggest snow I remember was the big centennial snow. Oh, that's been years ago. The snow was so deep you couldn't get out of the house. The boys had to take the shovel and the hoe and keep the snow raked away from around the door.

"There was a big old oak tree that stood in the corner of the yard. People say that tree was a hundred years old. We could not get no wood, so master had the boys to cut the big old oak tree for wood.

"Rabbits had a scant time. The boys would go out and track six or eight rabbits at a time. We had rabbits of all descriptions. We had rabbits for breakfast, rabbits for dinner, rabbits for supper time. We had fried rabbits, baked rabbits, stewed rabbits, boiled rabbits. Had rabbits, rabbits, rabbits the whole six or eight weeks the snow stayed on the ground.

"I remember when I was about twelve years old a woman had two small children. She went away from home and for fear that the children would get hurt on the outside she put them in the house and locked the door. In some way they got a match and struck it and the house caught fire. All the neighbors were a long ways off and by the time they reched the house it had fallen in. Finally the mother came and looked for her children and asked the neighbors did they save them. They said no, they did not know they were in the house. In fact they were too late anyway. So the fire was still hot and they had to wait for the ashes to cool and when the ashes got cool they went looking for the children and found the burned buttons that were on their little clothes, so they began raking around in the ashes and at last found each of their little hearts that had not burned, but the little hearts were still jumping and the man who found the hearts picked them up in his hand and stood speechless. He became so nervous he could not move. Their little hearts just quivered. They let their hearts lay out for a couple of days and when they buried their hearts they was still jumpin'. That was a sad time. From that day to this day I never lock no one up in the house."

---

**Interviewer: Miss Irene Robertson**
**Person interviewed: Henry Andrew (Tip) Williams**
**Biscoe, Arkansas**
 **Age: Born in 1854, 86**

"I was born three and one-half miles from Jackson, North Carolina. I was born a slave. I was put to work at six years old. They started me to cleaning off new ground. I thinned corn on my knees with my hands. We planted six or seven acres of cotton and got four or five cents a pound. Balance we planted was something to live on. My master was Jason and Betsy Williams. He had a small plantation; the smaller the plantation the better they was to their slaves.

"Jim Johnson's farm joined. He had nine hundred ninety-nine niggers. It was funny but every time a nigger was born one died. When he bought one another one would die. He was noted as having nine hundred ninety-nine niggers. It happened that way. He was rough on his place. He had a jail on his place. It was wood but close built. Couldn't get out of there. Put them in there and lock them up with a big padlock. He kept a male hog in the jail to tramp and walk over them. They said they kept them tied down in that place. Five hundred lashes and shot 'em up in jail was light punishment. They said it was light brushing. I lived up in the Piney Woods. It was big rich bottom plantations from Weldon Bridge to Halifax down on the river. They was rough on 'em, killed some. No, I never seen Jim Johnson to know him. He lived at Edenton, North Carolina. I recollect mighty well the day he died we had a big storm, blowed down big trees. That jail was standing when I come to Arkansas forty-seven years ago. It was a 'Bill brew' (stocks) they put men in when they put them in jail. Turned male hog in there for a blind.

"Part of Jim Johnson's overseers was black and part white. Hatterway was white and Nat was black. They was the head overseers and both bad men. I could hear them crying way to our place early in the morning and at night.

"Lansing Kahart owned grandma when I was a little boy.

"They took hands in droves one hundred fifty miles to Richmond to sell them. Richmond and New Orleans was the two big selling blocks. My uncle was sold at Richmond and when I come to Arkansas he was living at Helena. I never did get to see him but I seen his two boys. They live down there now. I don't know how my uncle got to Helena but he was turned loose down in this country at 'mancipation. They told me that.

"When a man wanted a woman he went and axed the master for her and took her on. That is about all there was to it. No use to want one of the women on Jim Johnson's, Debrose, Tillery farms. They kept them on their own and didn't want visitors. They was big farms. Kershy had a big farm.

"The Yankees never went to my master's house a time. The black folks knowd the Yankees was after freedom. They had a song no niggers ever made up, 'I wanter be free.'

"My master was too old to go to war but Bill went. I think it was better times in slavery than now but I'm not in favor of bringing it back on account of the cruelty and dividing up families. My master was good to us. He was proud of us. We fared fine. He had a five or six horse farm. His land wasn't strong but we worked and had plenty. Mother cooked for white and colored. We had what they et 'cepting when company come. When they left we got scraps. Then when Christmas come we had cakes and pies stacked up setting about for us to cut. They cut down through a whole stack of pies. Cut them in halves and pass them among us. We got hunks of cake a piece. We had plain eating er plenty all the time. You see I'm a big man. I wasn't starved out till I was about grown, after the War was over. Times really was hard. Hard, hard times come on us all.

"Mama got one whooping in her life. I seen that. Jason Williams whipped only two grown folks in my life, mama and my brother. Mama sassed her mistress or that what they called it then. Since then I've heard worse jawing not called sassing, call it arguing now. Sassing was a bad trait in them days. Brother was whooped in the field. He was seven years older than me. I didn't see none of that. They talked a right smart about it.

"The Williams was good to us all. Master's wife heired two women and a girl. Mama cooked, ironed, and worked in the field in time of a push (when necessary).

"I was hauling for the Rebel soldiers one rainy evening. It was dark and lightning every now and then. General Ransom was at the hotel porch when Sherman turned the bend one mile to come in the town. It was about four o'clock in the evening I judge. General Ransom's company was washing at Boom's Mill three miles. About one thousand men was out there cooking and in washing, resting. General Ransom went hollering, 'Yankees!' Went to his men. They got away I reckon. Sherman killed sixty men in that town I know. General Ransom went on his horse hollering, 'Yankees coming!' He went to his home eight miles from there. They went on through rough as could be.

"I hauled when it was so dark the team had to take me in home at night. My circuit was ten miles a day.

"My young master Bill Williams come in April soon as he got home and told us we was free but didn't have to leave. We stayed on and worked. He said he had nothing but the land and we had nothing. At the end of the year he paid off in corn and a little money. Us boys left then and mother followed us about. We ain't done no better since then. We didn't go far off.

"Forty-seven years ago I went to Weldon, North Carolina in a wagon, took the train to Gettysburg and from there come to Biscoe, Arkansas. I been about here ever since. Mr. Biscoe paid our way. We worked three years to pay him back. I cleared good money since I cone out here. I had cattle I owned and three head of horses all my own. Age crept up on me. I can't work to do much good now. I gets six dollars—Welfare money.

"Times is a puzzle to me. I don't know what to think. Things is got all wrong some way but I don't know whether it will get straightened out or not. Folks is making the times. It's the folks cause of all this good or bad. People not as good as they was forty years ago. They getting greedy."

---

**Interviewer: Miss Irene Robertson**
**Person interviewed: James Williams, Brinkley, Arkansas**
  **Age: 72**

"I come from close to Montgomery, Alabama. Man named John G. Elliott sent and got a number famlees to work his land. He was the richest man in them parts round Fryers Point, Mississippi. I was born after the Civil War. They used to say we what was raisin' up havin' so much easier time an what they had in slavery times. That all old folks could talk about. Said the onlies time the slaves had to comb their hair was on Sunday. They would comb and roll each others hair and the men cut each others hair. That all the time they got. They would roll the childerns hair or keep it cut short one. Saturday mornin' was the time the men had to curry and trim up the horses and mules. Clean out the lot and stalls. The women would sweep and scour the floors for Sunday.

"I haven't voted for a long time. It used to be some fun votin'. Din in Mississippi the whites vote one way and us the other. My father was a Republican. I was too.

"I have cataracts growing on my eyes. That hinders my work now. I got a little garden. It help out. I ain't got no propety no kind.

"The young folks seem happy. I guess they gettin' long fine. Some folks jes' lucky bout gettin' ahead and stayin' ahead. I can't tell no moren nothin' how times goiner serve this next generation they changein' all time seems lack. If the white folks don't know what goiner become of the next generation, they need not be asking a fellow lack me. I wish I did know.

"I ain't been on the PWA. I don't git no help ceptin' when I can work a little for myself."


**Interviewer: Samuel S. Taylor**
**Person interviewed: John Williams**
**County Hospital, ward 11, Little Rock, Arkansas**
 **Age: 75**


"I was born in 1863 in Texas right in the city of Dallas right in the heart of the town. After the War our owners brought us back to Little Rock. That is where they left from. They left here on account of the War. They run off their slaves to keep the Yankees from freeing them. All the old masters were dead. But the young ones were Louis Fletcher, John Fletcher, Dick Fletcher, Jeff Fletcher, and Len Fletcher. Five brothers of them. Their home was here in Little Rock. The War was going on. It went on four years and prior to the end of it I was born.

"My mother's name was Mary Williams. My father's name was John Williams. I was named after him.

"It is funny how they changed their names. Now, his name was John Scott before he went into the army. But after he went in, they changed his name into John Williams.

"His master's name was Scott but I don't know the other part of it. All five of the brothers was named for their mother's masters. She raised them. She always called all of them master. 'Cordin' to what I hear from the old folks, when one of them come 'round, you better call him master.

"In slave time, my father was a field hand, I know that. But I know more about my mother. I heard her say she was always a cook.

"I heard her speak about having cruel treatment from her first masters; I don't know who they were. But after the Fletchers bought them, they had a good time. They come all the way out of Louisiana up here. My mother was sold from her mother and sister-sold some two or three times. She never did get no trace of her sister, but she found her grandmother in Baton Rouge, Louisiana and brought her here. Her sister's name was Fannie and her grandmother's name was Crecie Lander. That is an Indian name. I couldn't understand nothing she would say hardly. She was bright. All my folks were bright but me. My mother had hair way down her shoulders and you couldn't tell my uncle from a dago. My grandmother was a regular Indian color. She spoke Indian too. You couldn't understand nothing she said.

"When I woke up, they had these homemade beds. I couldn't hardly describe them, but they put the sides into the posts with legs. They were stout things too what I am talkin' 'bout. They made cribs for us little children and put them under the bed. They would pull the cribs out at night and run them under the bed during the day. They called them cribs trundles. They called them trundles because they run them under the bed. For chairs and tables accordin' to what I heard my mother say, she was cook and they had everything in the big house and et pretty much what the white folks et. But we just had boxes in the cabins.

"Them that was in the white folks' house had pretty good meals, but them that was in the field they would feed just about like they would the hogs. They had little wooden trays and they would put little fat meat and pot-liquor and corn bread in the tray, and hominy and such as that. Biscuits came just on Sunday.

"They had old ladies to cook for the slave children and old ladies to cook for the hands. What was in the big house stayed in the big house. All the slave men ate in one place and all the slave women ate in one place. They weren't supposed to have any food in their homes unless they would go out foraging. Sometimes they would get it that way. They'd go out and steal ol' master's sweet potatoes and roast them in the fire. They'd go out and steal a hog and kill it. All of it was theirn; they raised it. They wasn't to say stealin' it; they just went out and got it. If old master caught them, he'd give 'em a little brushin' if he thought they wouldn't run off. Lots of times they would run off, and if he thought they'd run off because they got a whippin', he was kinda slow to catch 'em. If one run off, he'd tell the res', 'If you see so and so, tell 'im to come on back. I ain't goin' to whip 'im.' If he couldn't do nothin' with 'em, he'd sell 'em. I guess he would say to hisself, 'I can't do nothin' with this nigger. If I can't do nothing with 'im, I'll sell him and git my money outa him.'

"I have heard my mother say that some of the slaves that ran away would get destroyed by the wild animals and some of them would even be glad to come back home. Right smart of them got clean away and went to free states.

"After the War was over, they all was brought back here and the owners let them know they was free. They had to let them know they were free. I never heard my mother tell the details. I never heard her say just who brought her word or how it was told to her when they was freed.

"I never heard her say much about the church because she was a sinner. After they was freed, I would go many a night and set down in a corner where they was having a big dance.

"The pateroles and jayhawkers were bad. Many of them got hurt too. They tried to hurt the niggers and sometimes the niggers hurt them.

"Right after the War, my folks farmed for a living. They farmed on shares. They didn't have nothing of their own. They never did get nothing out of their work. I know they didn't get a thing. They farmed at first about seven miles out from Little Rock, below Fourche Dam on the Fletcher place. There ain't but one of the Fletchers living now, and that is Molly Daniels. She is old Louis Fletcher's daughter. All their brothers is dead. She's owning all the land now we used to till. It's over a thousand acres. She [HW: mother] stayed down there for about twenty or thirty years. Then she moved here to town. Here she cooked for white folks. My mother died about forty years ago—forty-two or three years; she's been dead sometime. My wife has been dead now for twelve years.

"I didn't get but a little schooling, for my father used to send me after the mules. One day the wheelbarrow had a load of bricks on it. It was upset. They had histed the bricks up on a high platform. It turned over as I was passing underneath, and one fell on me and struck my head. It was a long time after that before they would let me go to school again. After that I never got used to studying any more.

"My first teacher was Lottie Andrews (Charlotte Stephens). I had some more teachers too. Lemme see—Professor Fish was a white man. We had colored teachers under him. Then we had R.B. White. He was Reuben White's brother. R.B. White's wife was a teacher. Professor Fish was the superintendent. There ain't no truth to the tale that Reuben White was put in a coffin before he was dead. Reuben White built the First Baptist Church here and Milton White built a big church in Helena. They were brothers. Them was two sharp darkies.

"When I first started working, I drove teams. I raised crops a while and farmed. Then I left the country and come to town and got up to be a quarry man for years. Then I quit that and went to driving teams for the Merchant Transfer Company for years. Then I quit that and run on the road—the Mountain—for four years. Then I taken a coal chute on the Rock Island and run it for four years. Then I quit and went to working as an all-'round man in the shop. I stayed with them about nine years. Then I taken down in the shape that I am now.

"I have been out here to this hospital for twenty-four years going on twenty-five. Been down so that I couldn't hit a lick of work for twenty-five years. I have been in this building for eleven years. I get along tolerable fair. As the old man says, we can just live.

"I think the young people are going wild and if something isn't done to head them off pretty soon, they'll go too far. They ain't looking at what's going on up the road; they just call theirselves having a good time. They ain't looking to have nothing. They ain't looking to be nothing. They ain't looking to get nothing for the future. Don't know what they would do if they had to work part of the time for nothing like we did. I see men working now for ten dollars a month. I could take a fishing line and go fishing and beat that when I was young. Times is getting back almost as hard as they used to be.

"I am a Christian. I belong to Shiloh Baptist Church in North Little Rock. I helped build that church. Brother Hawkins was the pastor."

---

**Interviewer: Miss Irene Robertson**
**Person interviewed: Lillie Williams, Madison, Arkansas**
**Age: 69**

"I was born some place down in Mississippi. My papa's papa come from Georgia. He had a tar kiln; he cut splinters put them on it. It would smoke blackest smoke and drip for a week. He used it to grease the hubs of the wagons. We drunk pine tar tea for coughs. He split rails, made boards and shingles all winter. He had a draw-knife, a mall and wedges to use in his work. He learned that where he come from in Georgia. He sold boards, pailings when I can recollects. Grandma made tallow candles for everybody on our place in the fall when they killed the first yearling. They cooked up beeswax when they robbed bees. When I was a child I picked up pine knots for torches to quilt and knit by. We raised everything we lived on. I pulled sage grass to cure for brooms. Grandpa planted some broom corn and we swept the yards and lots with brooms made out of brush.

"Grandma kept a barrel to make locust and persimmon beer in. We dried apples and peaches all summer and put chinaberry seed 'mongst them to keep out worms.

"If we rode to church, it was in a steer wagon (ox wagon). Our oxen named Buck, Brandy Barley.

"Grandma raised me, two more girls, and a boy. Mama worked out. Our pa died. Mama worked 'mongst the white folks. Grandma was old-timey. She made our dresses to pick cotton in every summer. They was hot and stubby. They looked pretty. We was proud of them. Mama washed and ironed. She kept us clean, too. Grandma made us card and spin. I never could learn to spin but I was a good knitter. I could reel. I did love to hear it crack. That was a cut. We had a winding blade. We would fill the quills for our grandma to weave. Grandma was mighty quiet and particular. She come from Kenturkey. We all ploughed. I've ploughed and ploughed.

"I had three little children to raise and now I have nine grandchildren. I got five here now to look after when their mother is out at work. I have worked. We farmed in 1923 up till 1931 and got this house paid out. (Fairly good square-boxed, unpainted house—ed.)

"My mother-in-law was sold in Aberdeen, Mississippi on a tall stump. She clem up a ladder. Her ma was at the sale and said she was awful uneasy. But she was sold to folks close by. She could go to see her.

"Freedom come on. The colored folks slip about from place to place and whisper, 'We goiner be set free.' I think my mama left at freedom and come to twenty or twenty-two miles from Oxford, Mississippi. I don't know where I was born. But in Mississippi somewheres.

"There is something wrong about the way we are doing somehow. It is from hand to mouth. We buys too many paper sacks. They say work is hard to get. One thing now didn't used to be, you have to show the money before you can buy a thing. Seem like we all gone money crazy. Automobiles and silk stockings done ruined us all. White folks ought to straighten this out."

---

**Interviewer: Miss Irene Robertson**
**Person interviewed: Mary Williams, Clarendon, Arkansas**
**Age: Born 1872**
**Light color**

"My father was a slavery man two and one-half miles from Somerville, Tennessee. Colonel Rivers owned him. Argile Rivers was papa's name.

"He went to war. His job was hauling food to the soldiers. He lay out in the woods getting to his soldiers with provisions. He'd run hide under the feed wagon from the shot. Him and old master would be together sometimes. His master died, or was hurt and died after the War a long while.

"He said his master was good to him all time. They had to work hard. He raised one boy and me."

---

[HW: Ex-slave]

**Name of Interviewer: Irene Robertson**
**Subject: Ex-Slave—Herbs "Hant" experiences**
**Story:—Information**

**This information given by: Mary Williams**
**Place of Residence: Hazen, Arkansas**
**Occupation: Field Worker**
**Age: 69**

[TR: Information moved from bottom of first page.]

Mary Williams mother's name was Mariah and before she married her master forced her to go wrong and she had a son by him. They all called him Jim Rob. He was a mulatta. Then Mariah married Williams on General Garretts farm. The Rob Roy farm and the Garrett farm joined. Mary was born at Rob Roy, Arkansas near Humphrey. Mary said the master married her mother and father after her mother was stood up on a stump and auctioned off. Her mother was a house girl. Soon there were rumors of freedom but their family lived on where they were. Her father said when he was a boy he attended the draw bars and met the old master to get a ride up behind him.

Once when her father was real small he was eating biscuit with a hole in it made by a grown person sticking finger down in it, then fill the hole with molasses. That was a rarity they had just cooked molasses. He was sitting in front of the fire place. Big White Bobby stuck his nose and mouth to take a bite of his bread. He picked the cat up and threw it in the fire. The cat ran out, smutty, just flying. The old mistress came in there and got after him about throwing the cat in the fire.

One time when my father was going to see my mother. Before they got married, across the field. He had a bag of potatoes. He felt something, felt like some one had caught his bag and was pulling him back. He was much off a man and thought he could whip nearly every body around but he was too scared to run and couldn't hardly get away.

Mary's mother, Mariah two children had been gone off. They were coming in on the boat some time in the night. The master sent two of the big boys down to build a fire and wait at the landing till they came. They went in the wagon. There was an old empty house up on the hill. So they went up there and built a fire and put their quilts down for pallets by the fire place. They heard hants outside, they peeped out the log cracks. They saw something white out there all the doors were buttoned and propped. When the boat came it blew and blew. The master wondered what in the world was the matter down there. The captian said he hated to put them out and nobody to meet them. It was after midnight. So some of the boat crew built them a fire and next morning when they got up on the hill they noticed somebody asleep as they peeped through the cracks and called them. Saw their wagon and knew it too. They said they was afraid of them hants around the house, too afraid to go down to the boat landing if they did hear the boat. Hants can't be seen in daytime only by people "what born with veils over their faces."

Her father was going to mill to have corn ground. It was before day light. He was driving an ox wagon.

In front of him he saw a sweet maple limb moving up and down over the road in front of him. He went on and the ox butted and kicked at it and it followed them nearly to the mill. It sounded like somebody crying. It turned and went back still crying. Her father said there were hants up in the tree and cut the limb off and followed him carrying it between themselves so he couldn't see what they looked like.

It is a sign of death for a hoot owl to come hollow in your yard.

157

**Interviewer: Mrs. Bernice Bowden**
 **Person interviewed: Mary Williams**
**409 North Hickory, Pine Bluff, Arkansas**
 **Age: 82**

"Yes mam, I sure would be glad to talk to you 'bout slavery times. I can sure tell about it—I certainly can, lady.

"I am so proud 'bout my white folks 'cause they learned me how to work and tell the truth. I had a good master and mistress. Yes'm, I sure did.

"I was borned in middle Georgia and I just love the name of Georgia. I was the second born of 'leven children and they is all dead 'cept me—I'm the only one left to tell the tale.

"When the ginnin' started I was always glad 'cause I could ride the crank they had the mules hitched to. And then after the cotton was ginned they took it to the press and you could hear that screw go z-m-m-m and dreckly that 'block and tickle' come down. Yes mam, I sure did have good times.

"You ain't never seen a spinnin' wheel has you? Well, I used to card and spin. I never did weave but I hope dye the hanks. They weaved it into cloth and called it muslin.

"I can 'member all I want to 'bout the war. I 'member when the Yankees come through Georgia. I walked out in the yard with 'em and my white people just as scared of 'em as they could be. I heered the horses feet, then the drums, and then 'bout twenty-five or thirty bugles. I was so amazed when the Yankees come. I heered their songs but I couldn't 'member 'em.

"One thing I 'member jest as well as if 'twas this mornin'. That was the day young master Henry Lee went off to war. Elisha Pearman hired him to go and told him that when the war ceasted he would give him two or three darkies and let him marry his daughter. Young master Henry (he was just eighteen) he say he goin' to take old Lincoln the first thing and swing him to a limb and let him play around awhile and then shoot his head off. But I 'member the morning old mistress got a letter that told how young master Henry was in a pit with the soldiers and they begged him not to stick his head up but he did anyway and they shot it off. Old mistress jest cry so.

"One thing I know, the Yankees took a lot of things. I 'member they took Mrs. Fuller to the well and said they goin' hang her by the thumbs—but they just done it for mischievous you know. They didn't take nothin' from my white people 'cept some chickens and a hog, and cut down the hams. They put the old rooster in the sack and he went to squawkin' so they took him out and wrung his neck.

"My white people used to carry me with 'em anywhere they go. That's how come I learn so much. I sure did learn a heap when I was small. I 'member the first time my old mistress and my young mistress carried me to church. When the preacher got through preachin' (he was a big fine lookin' man with white gray hair) he come down from the pulpit and say 'Come to me, you sinners, poor and needy.' And he told what Jesus said to Nicodemus how he must be born again. I wanted to go to the mourners' bench so bad, but old mistress wouldn't let me. When I got home I told my mother to borned me again. You see I was jest little and didn't know no better.

"I never seen no Ku Klux but I could have. They never bothered us but they whipped the shirttails off some of 'em. Some darkies is the meanest things God ever put breath in.

"Most generally the white folks was good to their darkies. My young master used to sneak out his Blue Back Speller and learned my father how to read, and after the war he taught school. He started me off and then a teacher from the North come down and taught us.

"I've done pitty near every kind a work there is to do. There is some few white people here can identify me. I most always work for 'ristocratic people. It seems that was just my luck.

159

"I don't think nothin' of this here younger generation. They ain't nothin' to 'em. They say to me 'Why don't you have your hair straightened' but I say 'I've got along this far without painted jaws and straight hair.' And I ain't goin' wear my dresses up to my knees or trail 'em in the mud, either.

"I been married four times and every one of 'em is dead and buried. My las' husband was in the Spanish-American War and now I gets a pension. Yes'm it sure does help.

"I only had two children is all I is had. They is both dead and when God took my last one, I thought he wasn't jest but I see now God knows what's best cause if I had my grandchildren now I'd sure beat 'em. I'd love 'em, but I sure wouldn't let 'em run around.

"The biggest part of these niggers puts their mistakes on the white folks. It's easier to do right than wrong cause right whips wrong every time into a frazzle.

"I don't read much now since my eyes ain't so good but tell me whatever become of Teddy Roosevelt?

"I'm sorry I can't offer you no dinner but I'm just cookin' myself some peas.

"Well, lady, I sure am glad you come. I jest knew the Lord was goin' send somebody for me to talk to. I loves to talk so well. Good bye and come back again sometime."

---

**Interviewer: Mrs. Bernice Bowden**
**Person interviewed: Mary Williams**
   **409 Hickory, Pine Bluff, Arkansas**
**Age: 84**

[TR: Apparently a second interview with same person despite age discrepancy.]

"Yes ma'am, I know all about slavery. I'll be eighty-four the twenty-fifth of this month. I was born in 1855.

"My mother had eleven children and they all said I could remember the best of all. I'm the second oldest. And they all dead but me.

"I used to spin and on Friday I'd set aside my wheel and on Saturday morning we'd sweep yards. And Saturday evening was our holiday.

"I belonged to the Lees and my white folks was good to me. I was the aptest one among 'em, so they'd give me a basket and a ginger cake and I'd go to the Presly's after squabs. They'd be just nine days old 'cause they said if they was any older they'd be tough.

"Now, when the Yankees come through ever'body was up in the house 'cept me. I was out in the yard with the Yankees. No, I wasn't scared of 'em—I had better sense.

"This is all the 'joyment I have now is to think back in slavery times.

"In slavery times white folks used to carry me to church. They'd carry me to church in preference to anybody else. When they'd sing I'd be so happy I'd hop and skip. I'm one of the stewardess sisters of St. John's Methodist Church. We takes care of the sacrament table.

"I believe in visions. I'm a great revisionist. I don't have to be asleep either. Now if I see a vision of a black snake, it's a sign I got a black enemy. And if it's a light colored snake, it's a sign I got a white enemy. And if it's a kinda of a yellow snake, I got a enemy is a yellow nigger.

"Now, here's a true sign of death. If you dream of seen' nakedness, somebody sure goin' to die in your family or maybe your neighbors'.

"In slavery times they mostly wove their own dresses. Wove goods called muslin.

"And they wore bonnets in slavery times made out of bull rush grass. Called 'em bull rush bonnets. I knowed how to weave but they had me spinnin' all the time.

"I've always worked for the 'ristocrat white people—lawyers, doctors, and bankers. Mr. Frank Head was cashier of that old Merchant and Planters Bank. He was a northern man. Oh, from away up North.

"When I cooked, the greatest trouble I had was gettin' away. Nobody wanted me to leave. And I tell you those northern ladies wanted to call me Mrs. Williams. I'd say, 'Don't do that. You know these southern people don't like that—don't believe in that.' But you know she would call me Miss Mary. But I said, 'Don't do that.'

"I'm just an old darky and can't 'spress myself but I try to do what's right and I think that's the reason the Lord has let me live so long."

**Interviewer's Comment**

Husband was a soldier in the Spanish-American War and she receives a pension.

---

**Interviewer: Mrs. Bernice Bowden**
 **Person interviewed: Rosena Hunt Williams**
**R.F.D., Brinkley, Arkansas**
 **Age: 56**

"My mother was Amanda McVey. She was born two years, six months after freedom in Corinth, Mississippi. My father was born in slavery. Grandma lived with us at her death. Her name was Emily McVey. She was sold in her girlhood days. Uncle George was sold to a man in the settlement named Lee. His name was Joe Lee (Lea?). Another of my uncles was sold to a man named Washington. His name was George Washington. They were sold at different times. Being sold was their biggest dread. Some of them wanted to be sold trusting to be treated better.

"Mother and grandma didn't have a hard time like my father said he come up under. He said he was brought up hard. He was raised (reared) at Jackson, Tennessee. He was never sold. Master Alf Hunt owned him and his young master, Willie Hunt, inherited him. He said they never put him in the field till he was twelve years old. He started ploughing a third part of a day. A girl about grown and another boy a little older took turns to do a 'buck's' (a grown man) work. They was lotted of a certain tract and if it stay clear a certain time to get it all done. He said they got whooped and half fed. When the War was on, his white folks had to half feed their own selves. He talked like if the War had lasted much longer it would been a famine in the land. He hit this world in time to have a hard time of it. After freedom was worse time in his life.

"In August when the crops was laid by Master Hunt called them to the house at one o'clock by so many taps of the farm bell. It hung in a great big tree. He read a paper from his side porch telling them they free. They been free several months then and didn't a one of them know it."

**Interviewer: Miss Irene Robertson**
**Person interviewed: "Soldier" Williams, Forrest City, Arkansas**
**Age: 98**

"My name is William Ball Williams III. I was born in Greensburg. My owners was Robert and Mary Ball. They had four children I knowd. Old man Ball bought ma and two children for one thousand five hundred dollars. I never was sold. I want to live to be a hundred years old. I'm ninety-eight years old now.

"Ma was Margarett Ball. Pa was William Anderson. Ma was a cook and pa a field hand. They whooped a plenty on the place where I come up. Some of 'em run off. Some they tied to a tree. Bob Ball didn't use no dogs. When they got starved out they'd come outen the woods. Of course they would. Bob Ball raised fine tobacco, fine Negroes, fine horses. He made us go to church. Four or five of us would walk to the white folks' Baptist church. The master and his family rode. It was a good piece. We had dances in the cabins every once in a while. We dance more in winter time so we could turn a pot down in the door to drown out the noise. We had plenty plain grub to eat.

"I run away to Louisville to j'ine the Yankees one day. I was scared to death all the time. They put us in front to shield themselves. They said they was fighting for us—for our freedom. Piles of them was killed. I got a flesh wound. I'm scarred up some. We got plenty to eat. I was in two or three hot battles. I wanted to quit but they would catch them and shoot them if they left. I didn't know how to get out and get away. I mustered out at Jacksonville, Florida and walked every step of the way back. When I got back it was fall of the year. My folks still at my master's. I was on picket guard at Jacksonville, Florida. We fought a little at Pensacola, Florida.

"At the end of the War provisions got mighty scarce. If we didn't have enough to eat we took it. They hadn't raised nothing to eat the last two years. Before I got back to Kentucky the Ku Klux was about and it was hard to get enough to eat to keep traveling on. I was scared nearly to death all the time. I'm not in favor of war. I didn't stay on with the master but my folks lived on. They didn't want to hire Negro soldiers. I traveled about hunting a good place and got to Osceola, Arkansas. I been here in Forrest City twenty ard years. The best people in the world live in Arkansas.

"I'm going to try to go to the Yankee Reunion. They sent me a big letter (invitation). They going to send me a ticket and pay all my expenses. It is at Gettysburg. It is from June 29th to July 6th. My grandson is going to take care of me.

"I get one hundred dollars a month pension. It keeps us mighty well. I want to live to be a hundred years old."

---

**Interviewer: Miss Irene Robertson**
**Person interviewed: Anna Williamson, Holly Grove, Arkansas**
**Age: Between 75 and 80**

"Grandma come from North Carolina. Her master was Rodes Herndon, then Cager Booker. He owned my mama. My name is Anna Booker. I married Wes Williamson.

"My papa's master was Calvin Winfree. He come from Virginia. Me and Bert Winfree (white) raised together close to Somerville, Tennessee.

"Grandma and grandpa was named Maria and Allen. Her master was Rodes Herndon. I was fourth to the oldest of mama's children. She give me to grandma. That who raised me. Mama took to the field after freedom. Mama had seven or eight children.

"Mama muster been a pretty big sorter woman when she young. A ridin' boss went to whoopin' her once and she tore every rag clothes he had on offen him. I heard em say he went home strip start naked. I think they said he got turned off or quit, one.

"When mama was in slavery she had three girl babies and long wid them she nursed some of the white babies. She cooked some but wasn't the regular white folks' cook. Another black woman was the regular cook. I heard her say she was a field hand mostly durin' slavery.

"Folks was free two or three years fore they knowed it. Nobody told em.

"I used to have to go up the road to get milk for the old mistress. She boxed my ears. That when I was a child reckly after the war.

"They had a latch and a hart bar cross the door. I never was out but once after dark. I never seen no Ku Klux. My folks didn't know they was free.

"Dr. Washington lived in Somerville, Tennessee and brought us to Arkansas to farm. He owned acres and acres of land here. I was grown and had a house full of children. I got five living now.

"I don't vote. I don't know who to vote for. I would vote for the worst kinder officers maybe and I wouldn't wanter make times harder on us all 'an they is.

"I been cookin' and farmin' all my life. Now I get $10 a month from the Sociable Welfare.

"I used to pick up chips at Mrs. Willforms—pick up a big cotton basket piled up fore I quit. I seen the Yankees, they camped at the fair grounds. I thought they wore the prettiest clothes and the brass buttons so pretty on the blue suits. I hear em beat the drum. I go peep out when they come by.

"My old mistress slapped me till my eye was red cause one day I says 'Ain't them men pretty?' They camped at what is now the Fair Grounds at Somerville, Tennessee, at sorter right of town. My papa was a ox driver. That is all he done bout. Seem like there was haulin' to be done all the time.

"The folks used to be heap better than they is now. Some of the masters was mean to the slaves but they mortally had plenty to eat and wear and a house to

166

live in. Some of the houses was sorry and the snow come in the cracks but we had big fire places and plenty wood to cook and keep warm by. The children all wore flannel clothes then to keep em warm. They raised sheep.

"It is a shame what folks do now. These young darky girls marries a boy and they get tired each other. They quit. They ain't got no sign of divorce! Course they ain't never been married! They jes' take up and live together, then they both go on livin' with some other man an' woman. It ain't right! Folks ain't good like they used to be. We old folks ain't got no use for such doin's. They done too smart to be told by us old folks. I do best I can an' be good as I knows how to be.

"The times is fine as I ever seen in my life. I wish I was young and strong. I wouldn't ask nobody for sistance. Tey ain't nuthin' wrong wid this year's crop as I sees. Times is fine."

---

**Interviewer: Miss Irene Robertson**
**Person interviewed: Callie Halsey Williamson, Biscoe, Arkansas**
  **Age: 60?**

"Mother was born in Alabama during slavery. Her name was Levisa Halsey. Neither of my parents were sold. Mother was tranferred (transferred) to her young mistress. She had no children and still lived in the home with her people. Her mother, Emaline, was the cook. Master Bradford owned grandmother and grandfather both and my own father all. Mother was the oldest and only child.

"I don't know whether they was mean to all the slaves or not. Seems they were not to my folks. The old man died sometime before freedom. The young master went to get a overseer. He brought a new man to take his own place. He whooped grandma and auntie and cut grandma's long hair off with his pocket-knife.

"During that time grandpa slip up on the house top and take some boards off. Grandma would sit up in her bed and knit by moonlight through the hole. He had to put the boards back. She had to work in the field in daytime.

"During the War they were scared nearly to death of the soldiers and would run down in their master's big orchard and hide in the tall broom sage. They rode her young master on a rail and killed him. A drove of soldiers come by and stopped. They said, 'Young man, can you ride a young horse?' They gathered him and took him out and brought him in the yard. He died. They hurt him and scared him to death.

"Another train come and loaded up all the slaves and somehow when freedom come on, my folks was here at Arkadelphia. They said they lived in fear of the soldiers all the time.

"Mother said a woman come first and stuck a flag out a upstairs window and the Yankees shot the guns off and some of them made talks on freedom to the Negroes and white folks. They seen that at Arkadelphia.

"Mama, grandma, and grandpa started on their way back home following soldier camps. They never got back to their homes. They never did like the Yankees and grieved about the way they done their young master. He was like one of my father's own children. They seen hard times after freedom. It was hard to live and they was used to work but they had a good living. They had to die in Arkansas. How come I'm here now."

---

**Interviewer: Miss Irene Robertson**
**Person interviewed: Charlotte Willis, Madison, Arkansas**
**Age: 63**

"Grandpa said he walked every step of the way from old Virginia to Mississippi. They camped at night, cooked and fed them. They didn't eat no more till they camped next night. They was walked in a peart pace and the guards and traders rode. They stop every now and then for to be cried off and some more be took on.

"Grandpa said he didn't wanter be sold but they never ax 'em no diffurence. Sold 'em and took 'em right along. They better keep their feelings hid, for them traders was same kind er stock these cattle men is today judging from the way he say it was then. Grandpa loved Virginia long as he have breath in him.

"We used to sing

'Old Virginia nigger say he love hot mush;
 Alabama nigger say, good God, nigger, hush.'

(She sang it very fast and in a fashion Negroes only can do—ed.) He wore a big straw hat and he'd get up and fan us out the way.

"Grandma was brought from South Carolina by the Willises to Mississippi. I heard her say her and him was made to jump over the broom. Called that getting 'em married. Grandpa said that was the way white folks had of showing off the couples. Then it would be 'nounced from the big house steps they was man and wife. Sometimes more than two be 'nounced at the gatherin'.

"They had good times sometimes. They talked 'bout corn shuckings, corn shellings, cotton traumpin's, (packing cotton in wagon beds by walking on it over and over, she said—ed.) and dances.

"Mother said she never was sold. She b'long to the Willises in Mississippi.

"I reckon I sure do 'members my grandpa and grandma bof. Seventeen of us all lived at Grandpa Wash Hollivy's home. He was paying on it and died. The house have three rooms in it. In the fall of the year grandma took all the rancid grease and skins and get the drippings from the ash hopper and make soap 'nough to do 'er till sometime next year. She made it in the iron washpot. He raised meat to do us till sometime next year. We never run short on nothing to eat.

"We never had but 'bout two dresses at the same time. When I come on, dresses was scarce. If we tore our dresses, we wore patches. We was sorter 'shamed to have our dresses patched up.

"I heard 'em say grandpa's house was guarded to keep off the Ku Kluck one night. They come all right 'nough but went to another house. They started whooping. The guards left grandpa's house and went down there and shot into them. Some of them was killed and the horses run off. Some run off quick and got out the way. I never caught on to what they guarded grandpa for.

"I had one girl baby what died. I been married once in my life. We rents our house. I never 'plied to the Welfare yit. We been farming my enduring life. Still farming; I says we is.

"Old folks give out and can't run on wid the work. Young folks no 'count and works to sorter git by their own selfs. Way I see it. We got so far off the track and can't git back. Starve 'fore we git back like we used to be. We used to git credit. Now there ain't no place to git it. We down and can't git up. Way I sees it. Young generation is so uneasy, ain't still a minute. They wanter be going all the time. They don't marry; they goes lives together. Then they quits and take up wid somebody else. I don't know what make 'em do thater way. That the way the right young ones doing now.

"My pa looked on me when I was three days old and left us. I ain't never seen him since."

---

**Interviewer: Samuel S. Taylor**
**Person interviewed: Ella Wilson**
**1611 McGowan Street, Little Rock, Arkansas**
**Age: Claims 100**

"I was born in Atlanta, Georgia. I don't remember the month. But when the Civil War ceased I was here then and sixteen years old. I'm a hundred years old. Some folks tries to make out like it ain't so. But I reckon I oughter know.

"The white folks moved out from Georgia and went to Louisiana. I was raised in Louisiana, but I was born in Georgia. I have had several people countin' up my age and they all say I is a hundred years old. I had eight children. All of them are free born. Four of them died when they were babies. I lost one just a few days ago.

"I had such a hard time in slavery. Them white folks was slashing me and whipping me and putting me in the buck, till I don't want to hear nothin' about it.

"An old man named Dr. Polk got a dime from me and said it was for the Old Age Pension. He lived in Magnolia, Arkansas. They ran him out of Magnolia for ruining a colored girl and I don't know where he is now. I know he got ten cents from me.

"The first work I ever did was nursing the white children. My old mis' called me in the house and told me that she wanted me to take care of her children and from then till freedom came, I stayed in the house nursing. I had to get up every morning at five when the cook got up and make the coffee and then I had to go in the dining-room and set the table. Then I served breakfast. Then I went into the house and cleaned it up. Then I 'tended to the white children and served the other meals during the day. I never did work in the fields much. My old mars said I was too damned slow.

"They carried me out to the field one evening. He never did show me nor tell me how to handle it and when I found myself, he had knocked me down. When I got up, he didn't tell me what to do, but when I picked up my things and started droppin' the seeds ag'in, he picked up a pine root and killed me off with it. When I come to, he took me up to the house and told his wife he didn't want me into the fields because I was too damned slow.

"My mars used to throw me in a buck and whip me. He would put my hands together and tie them. Then he would strip me naked. Then he would make me squat down. Then he would run a stick through behind my knees and in front of my elbows. My knees was up against my chest. My hands was tied together just in front of my shins. The stick between my arms and my knees held me in a squat. That's what they called a buck. You could [TR: sic: couldn't] stand up an' you couldn't git your feet out. You couldn't do nothin' but just squat there and take what he put on you. You couldn't move no way at all. Just try to. You jus' fall over on one side and have to stay there till you turned over by him.

"He would whip me on one side till that was sore and full of blood and then he would whip me on the other side till that was all tore up. I got a scar big as the place my old mis' hit me. She took a bull whip once—the bull whip had a piece

172

of iron in the handle of it—and she got mad. She was so mad she took the whip and hit me over the head with the butt end of it, and the blood flew. It ran all down my back and dripped off my heels. But I wasn't dassent to stop to do nothin' about it. Old ugly thing! The devil's got her right now!! They never rubbed no salt nor nothin' in your back. They didn't need to.

"When the war come, they made him serve. He would go there and run away and come back home. One day after he had been took away and had come back, he was settin' down talkin' to old mis', and I was huddled up in the corner listenin', and I heered him tell her, 'Tain't no use to do all them things. The niggers'll soon be free.' And she said, 'I'll be dead before that happens, I hope.' And she died just one year before the slaves was freed. They was a mean couple.

"Old mars used to strip my sister naked and make her lay down, and he would lift up a fence rail and lay it down on her neck. Then he'd whip her till she was bloody. She wouldn't get away because the rail held her head down. If she squirmed and tried to git loose, the rail would choke her. Her hands was tied behind her. And there wasn't nothin' to do but jus' lay there and take it.

"I am almost a stranger here in Little Rock. My father was named Lewis Hogan and I had one sister named Tina and one named Harriet. His white folks what he lived with was Mrs. Thomas. He was a carriage driver for her. Pleas Collier bought him from her and took him to Louisiana. All the people on my mother's side was left in Georgia. My grandmother's name was Rachel. Her white folks she lived with was named Dardens. They all lived in Atlanta, Georgia. I remember the train we got on when we left Georgia. Grandma Rachel had one daughter named Siney. Siney had a son named Billie and a sister named Louise. And my grandmother was free when I first got big enough to know myself. I don't know how come she was free. That was a long time before the war. The part of Georgia we lived in was where chestnuts grow, but they wasn't no chinkapins. All my grandmother's people stayed in Atlanta, and they were living at the time I left there.

"My mother's name was Dinah Hogans and my father's name was Lewis Hogans. I don't know where they were borned. But when I knowed him, they was in Georgia. My mother's mars bought my father 'cause my mother heard that Collier was goin' to break up and go to Louisiana. My father told his mars that if he

173

(Collier) broke up and left, he never would be no more good to him. Then my mother found out what he said to Collier, so she told her old mis' if Collier left, she never would do her no more good. You see, my mother was give to Mrs. Collier when old Darden who was Mrs. Collier's father died. So Collier bought my father. Collier kept us all till we all got free. White folks come to me sometimes about all that.

"You jus' oughter hear me answer them. I tells them about it just like I would colored folks.

"'Them your teeth in your mouth?'

"'Whose you think they is? Suttinly they're my teeth.'

"'Ain't you sorry you free?'

"'What I'm goin' to be sorry for? I ain't no fool.'

"'How old is you?'

"I tells them. Some of 'em want to argue with me and say I ain't that old. Some of 'em say, 'Well, the Lawd sure has blessed you.' Sure he's blessed me. Don't I know that?

"I've seen 'em run away from slavery. There was a white man that lived close to us who had just one slave and he couldn't keep him out the woods to save his soul. The white man was named Jim Sales and the colored boy was named— shucks, I can't remember his name. But I know Jim Sales couldn't keep that nigger out the woods nohow.

"I was freed endurin' the Civil War. We was in at dinner and my old mars had been to town. Old man Pleas Collier, our mean mars, called my daddy out and then he said, 'All you come out here.' I said to myself, 'I wonder what he's a goin' to do to my daddy,' and I slipped into the front room and listened. And he said, 'All of you come.' Then I went out too. And he unrolled the Government paper he had in his hand and read it and told us it meant that all of us was free. Didn't tell us we was free as he was. Then he said the Government's going to send you some money to live on. But the Government never did do it. I never did see nobody that got it. Did you? They didn't give me nothin' and they didn't give my father nothin'. They just sot us free and turned us loose naked.

"Right after they got through reading the papers and told us we was free, my daddy took me to the field and put me to work. I'd been workin' in the house before that.

"Then they wasn't payin' nobody nothin'. They just hired people to work on halves. That was the first year. But we didn't get no half. We didn't git nothin'. Just time we got our crop laid by, the white man run us off and we didn't get nothin'. We had a fine crop too. We hadn't done nothin' to him. He just wanted all the crop for hisself and he run us off. That's all.

"Well, after that my daddy took and hired me out up here in Arkansas. He hired me out with some old poor white trash. We was livin' then in Louisiana with a old white man named Mr. Smith. I couldn't tell what part of Louisiana it was no more than it was down there close to Homer, about a mile from Homer. My mother died and my father come and got me and took me home to take care of the chillen.

"I have been married twice. I married first time down there within four miles of Homer. I was married to my first husband a number of years. His name was Wesley Wilson. We had eight children. My second husband was named Lee somepin or other. I married him on Thursday night and he left on Monday morning. I guess he must have been taking the white folks' things and had to clear out. His name was Lee Hardy. That is what his name was. I didn't figure he stayed with me long enough for me to take his name. That nigger didn't look right to me nohow. He just married me 'cause he thought I was a working woman and would give him money. He asked me for money once but I didn't give 'im none. What I'm goin' to give 'im money for? That's what I'd like to know.

"After my first husband died, I cooked and went on for them white folks. That was the only thing I could do. I was cooking before he died. I can't do no work now. I ain't worked for more than twenty years. I ain't done no work since I left Magnolia.

"I belong to the Collins Street Baptist Church—Nichols' church.

"I don't git no pension. I don't git nothin'. I been down to see if I could git it but they ain't give me nothin' yit. I'm goin' down ag'in when I can git somebody to carry me."

## Interviewer's Comment

Ella Wilson insists that she is one hundred years old and that she was born sixteen years before freedom. The two statements conflict. From her appearance and manner, either might be true.

---

## Interviewer: Mrs. Bernice Bowden
## Person interviewed: Robert Wilson
## 811 West Pullen Street, Pine Bluff, Arkansas
## Age: 101

"My name is Robert Wilson. I was born in Halifax County, Virginia. How old am I? Accordin' to my recollection I was twenty-three years old befo' the war started. Old master tole me how old I was. I'm a hundred and one now. Yes'm I *knows* I am.

"Yes'm I been sold. They put us up on the auction block jest like we was a hoss. They put me up and white man ax 'Who want to buy this boy?' One man say 'ten dollars' and then they run it up to a hundred. And they buy a girl to match you and raise you up together. When you want to get married you jump over the broomstick. I used to weigh one hundred and fifty-six pounds and a half, standin' weight. I could pick four and five hundred pounds of cotton in a day.

"When the Yankees come, old master make us boys take the sack of money and hide it in the big pond. Yes'm, we drove the buggy right in the water.

"Durin' the time of the war I used to ride 'long side of the Yankees. They give me a blue coat with brass buttons and a blue cap and brass-toed boots. I used to saddle and curry the bosses. I member Company Fifth and Sixth.

"They tole us the war was to make things better. We didn't know we was free till 'bout six months after the war was over. I didn't care whether I was free or not.

"'Bout slavery—well, I thinks like this. I think they fared better then. They didn't have to worry 'bout spenses. We had plenty chicken and everything. Nowdays when you pay the rent you ain't got nothin' left to buy somethin' to eat.

"Yes'm, I been to school. I'se a preacher (showing me his certificate of ordination). I lives close to the Lord. The Lord done left me here for a purpose.

"When we used to pray we put our heads under the wash pot to keep old master from hearin' us. Old master make us put the chillun to bed fo' dark. I 'member one song he make us sing—

'Down in Mobile, down in Mobile
 How I love dat pretty yellow gal,
 She rock to suit me--;
 Down in Mobile, down in Mobile.'

"You 'member when Grant took the fort at Vicksburg? I 'member he and that general on the white hoss—yes'm, General Lee, they eat dinner together and then after dinner they go to fightin'.

"Oh lord! Don't talk about them Ku Klux.

"Cose I believes in spirits. Don't you? Well you ain't never been skeered.

"After freedom my folks refugeed from Virginia to Tennessee so I went to Memphis. We got things from the Bureau. Yes, Lord! I had everything I wanted. I wouldn't care if that time would come back now.

"'Did you ever vote?' Me? Yes'm I voted. Never had no trouble 'tall. I voted for Garfield. I 'member when Garfield was shot. I was settln' out in the yard. The moon was in the 'clipse. I'll never forget it.

"I think the colored folks should have a legal right to vote, cause if ever they come another war—now listen—them darkies ain't never goin' to France again. The nigger ain't got no country—this is white man's town.

"What I been doin' since the war? Well, I'm a good cook. When I puts on the white apron, I knows what to do. Then I preaches. The Lord done revealed things to me.

"I'll tell you 'bout this younger generation. They is goin' to destruction. They is not envelopin (developing) their education.

"Well I done tole you all I know. Guess I tole you 'bout a book, ain't I?"

---

## Interviewer: Mrs. Bernice Bowden
### Person interviewed: Tom Windham, 723 Missouri, Pine Bluff, Arkansas
### Age: 98

"I was twenty-one years old when the war was settled. My mother and my grandmother kep' my age up and after the death of them I knowed how to handle it myself.

"My old master's name was Butler and he was pretty fair to his darkies. He give em plenty to eat and wear.

"I was born and raised in Indian Territory and emigrated from there to Atlanta, Georgia when I was about twelve or thirteen. We lived right in Atlanta. I cleaned up round the house. Yes ma'm, that's what I followed. When the Yankees come to Atlanta they just forced us into the army. After I got into the army and got used to it, it was fun—just like meat and bread. Yankees treated me good. I was sorry when it broke up. When the bugle blowed we knowed our business. Sometimes, the age I is now, I wish I was in it. Father Abraham Lincoln was our President. I knowed the war was to free the colored folks. I run away from my white folks is how come I was in the Yankee army. I was in the artillery. That deefened me a whole lot and I lost these two fingers on my left hand—that's all of my joints that got broke.

"Before the war my white folks was good to us. I had a better time than I got now.

"My father and mother was sold away from me, but old mistress couldn't rest without em and went and got em back. They stayed right there till they died. Us folks was treated well. I think we should have our liberty cause us ain't hogs or horses—us is human flesh.

"When I was with the Yankees, I done some livin'.

"I went to school two months in my life. I should a gone longer but I found where I could get next to a dollar so I quit. If I had education now it might a done me some good.

"I used to be in a brass band. I like a brass band, don't make no difference where I hear it.

"There was one song we played when I was in the army. It was:

'Rasslin Jacob, don't weep
 Weepin' Mary, don't weep.
 Before I'd be a slave
 I'd be buried in my grave,
 Go home to my father and be saved.'

The Rebels was hot after us then. Another one we used to sing was:

'My old mistress promised me
 When she die, she'd set me free.'

"After the war I continued to work around the white folks and yes ma'm, I seen the Ku Klux many a time. They bothered me sometimes but they soon let me alone. They was a few Yankees about and they come together and made the Ku Klux stay in their place.

"One time after the war I went to Ohio and stayed three months but it was too cold for me. Man I worked for was named Harper and as good a man as ever broke a piece of bread.

"I come back South and learned how to farm. I been here in this country of Arkansas a long time. I hoped clean up this place (Pine Bluff) and make a town of it.

"I got a daughter and two sisters alive in Africa today—in Liberia. I went there after we was free. I liked it. Just the thoughts of bein' where Christ traveled—that's the good part of it. They furnished us transportation to go to Africa after the war and a lot of the colored folks went. I come back cause I had a lot of kin here, but I sent my daughter and two sisters there and they're alive there today."

---

**FOLKLORE SUBJECTS**
 **Interviewer: Bernice Bowden**
 **Subject: Apparitions**

**Information by: Tom Windham**
 **Place of Residence: 723 Missouri St. Pine Bluff, Ark.**
 **Occupation: None (Age 92)**

[TR: Information moved from bottom of first page.]
 [TR: Same name, address, six year age difference from last informant.]

"Yes ma'm, I believe in spirits—you got two spirits—one bad and one good, and when you die your bad spirit here on this earth.

Now my mother comes to see me once in awhile at night. She been dead till her bones is bleached, but she comes and tells me to be a good boy. I always been obedient to old and young. She tell me to be good and she banish from me.

My grandmother been to see me once.

Old Father Abraham Lincoln, I've seen him since he been dead too. I got a gun old Father Abraham give me right out o' his own hand at Vicksburg. I'm goin' to keep it till I die too.

Yes ma'm, I know they is spirits."

---

**Pine Bluff District**
**FOLKLORE SUBJECTS**
**Interviewer: Martin - Barker**
**Subject: Ex-Slave**
**Story.**

**Information by: Tom Windham**
**Place of Residence: 1221 Georgia St.**
**Age: 87**

[TR: Information moved from bottom of first page.]

My master was an Indian. Lewis Butler of Oklahoma. I was born and raised in Muskogee, Okla.

All of marse Butler's people were Creek Indians. They owned a large plantation and raised vegetables. They lived in tepees, had floors and were set on a lot and a wall boarded up around them. This was done so that they could hide the slaves they had stolen.

I was twelve or thirteen years old, when the Indians had a small war. They wouldn't allow us to fight. If we did, we were punished. They had a place and made us work. I went to school two months also a little at night. Cant read nor write. I am all alone now here in America. I have a daughter in Ethiopia, teaching school, also two sisters.

I served in several wars and I have been to Ethiopia. We left Monroe, La., took water, then went back by gun-boat to Galveston. The Government took us over and brought us back. After the Civil war was over the Indians let the slaves go.

I had an Indian wife and wore Indian dress and when I went to Milford, Tenn., I had to send the outfit home to Okla. I had long hair until 1931.

My Indians believed in our God. They held their meetings in a large tent. They believed in salvation and damnation, and in Heaven and Hell.

My idea of Heaven is that it is a holy place with God. We will walk in Heaven just as on earth. As in him we believe, so shall we see.

The earth shall burn, and the old earth shall pass away and the new earth will be created. The saints will return and live on, that is the ones who go away now.

The new earth is when Jesus will cone to earth and reign. Every one has two spirits. One that God kills and the other an evil spirit. I have had communication with my dead wife twice since I been in Pine Bluff. Her spirit come to me at night, calling me, asking whar wuz baby?

That meant our daughter whut is across the water.

My first wifes name was Arla Windham. My second wife was just part Indian. I have seen spirits of friends just as they were put away. I shore believe in ghosts. Their language is different from ours. I knew my wife's voice cause she called me "Tommy".

---

**Interviewer: Mrs. Bernice Bowden**
**Person interviewed: Alice Wise**

**1112 Indiana Street, Pine Bluff, Arkansas**
**Age: 79**

"I was born in South Carolina, and I sent and got my age and the man sent me my age. He said he remembered me. He said, 'You married Marcus Wise. I know you is seventy-nine 'cause I'm seventy-four and you're older'n me. Why, I got a boy fifty-three years old.

"We belonged to Daniel Draft. His wife was named Maud. And my father's people was named Wesley Caughman and his wife was Catherine Caughman.

"I can recollect hearin' the folks hollerin' when the Yankees come through and singin' this old cornfield song

'I'm a goin' away tomorrow
 Hoodle do, hoodle do.'

That's all I can recollect.

"I can recollect when we moved from the white folks. My father driv' a wagon and hauled lumber to Columbia from Lexington.

"I don't know how old I was when I come here. My age got away from me, that's how come I had to write home for it, but I had three chillun when I come to this country; I know that.

"I went to school a little, but chillun in them days had to work. I was always apt about washin' and ironin' and sewin' and so if anybody was stopped from school I was stopped. I used to set pockets in pants for mama. In them days they weaved and made their own.

"They'd do better if they had a factory here now. Things wouldn't be so high.

"Oh Lord, yes, I could knit. I'd sit up some nights and knit a half a sock and spin and card.

"My mother's boys would card and spin a broach when they wasn't doin' nothin' else, but nowadays you can't get 'em to bring you a bucket of water.

"They say they is weaker and wiser, but I say they is weaker and foolisher. That's what I think. You know they ain't like the old folks was. Folks works nowadays and keeps their chillun in school till they're grown, and it don't do 'em much good-some of 'em."

---

**Interviewer: Samuel S. Taylor**
 **Person interviewed: Frank Wise, 1006 Victory Street,**
   **Little Rock, Arkansas**
 **Age: 81 to 85**

### Birth and Parents

"I was born in Burch County, Georgia, in 1854. I came to this state in 1871; I think I was about sixteen years old then.

"My father was named Jim Wise and my mother was named Harriet Wise. My father belonged to the Wises, and my mother to the Crawfords. They didn't live on the same plantation. When they married, she was a Crawford. Her old master was named Jim Crawford. I don't know how she and my father happened to meet up. Wise and Crawford had adjoining plantations. Both of them was in Burch County. My father's father was named Jacob Wise and his mother was named Martha. I don't remember the names of their master. I don't remember the names of my mother's people.

## War Memories

"I remember the year the War ended. I remember when the Yankees came on the place that day the War ended. We children was all settin' out in the yard. Some of them ran under the house when they saw the soldiers. They were shooting the chickens and everything, taking the horses, and anything else they thought they could use. They said to the old lady, 'Lemme kill them little niggers.' Old miss said, 'No, wait till you set them free.' He said, 'No, when we set them free, we ain't goin' to kill them.' They got around in the house, under the house, and in the yard. They asked the old lady, 'Where is the horses?' She said, 'I don't know.' They said, 'Go down in the woods and get them.' Somebody went down and brought back a mare and a mule and a colt. They knocked the colt in the head and shot him. They took the mare and the mule. They took all the meat out of the smokehouse. They didn't set us free, and they didn't tell us anything about freedom. Not then.

## How Freedom Came

"I don't remember how we got the news of freedom. I don't remember what the slaves expected to get. I don't know what they got, if they got anything. I don't remember nothin' about that.

## Schooling

"I went to school about eight days. That's all the schooling I ever got. I had a brother and sister who went to school, but I never went much. I went to school what little I did right here in Lonoke County, Arkansas. My teacher was Tom Fuller. He was a colored man. He came from down in Texas. I learned everything I know by watching people and listenin' to them.

## Occupational Experiences

"The first thing I ever did was farming. I farmed all up till 1879. I worked on steamboat till 1881, and then I went out railroading. I worked at that a long time. I married in 1883. I was about twenty-seven years old then, and a few months over.

"While I was farming, I did some sharecropping, but I never got cheated out of anything.

## Ku Klux

"I remember the folks had been off to see their people and the Ku Klux taken the stock while they were gone. I don't remember the Ku Klux Klan interfering with the Negroes much. I never saw them.

## Voting

"I never voted till Cleveland began his campaign for President. I voted for eight presidents. Nobody ever bothered me about it.

## Family

"There were six children in my mother's family. My father had six brothers. He made the seventh. I had nine children in all. Four of them are living now. One is here; one, in St. Louis; and two, in Chicago. My boy is in Chicago.

## Opinions

"The majority of the young people are just growing up. Lots of them are not getting any raising at all."

## Interviewer's Comment

Wise is between eighty-one and eighty-five years old. The data he gives conflict, some of it indicating the earlier and some of it later years.

He doesn't talk much and has to be pumped. He doesn't lose the thread of the discourse. His failure to talk on details of his early life seem to the interviewer due to unwillingness rather than lack of memory. While his age is advanced, his mind is sharp for one who has had such limited training.

He has no definite means of support, but states that he has been promised a pension in September--he means old age assistance.

---

**Interviewer: Miss Irene Robertson**
**Person interviewed: Lucy Withers, Brinkley, Arkansas**
**Age: 86**

I was born 5-1/2 miles from Abbeville, South Carolina, in sight of Little Mountain. I do remember the Civil War. I never seen them fight. They come to about twenty or thirty miles from where I lived. They didn't bother much in the parts where I lived. All the white men folks went to war. My mama's master was

Edward Roach and his wife was Miss Sarah Roach. My papa's master was Peter Radcliff and Miss Nancy Radcliff. They give me to her niece, Miss Jennie Shelitoe. When she married she wanted me. After freedom I married. In 1866 we come to a big farm close to Pine Bluff. Then we lived close to Memphis and I been living here in Brinkley a long time.

The Ku Klux put down a Governor in South Carolina right after the war. They rode everywhere night and day scaring everybody. They wouldn't let no colored people hold office. That governor was a colored man. The Ku Klux whipped both black and white folks. They run the Yankees plumb out er that country.

No sir ree I never voted and I ain't never goner vote! Women is tearing dis world up.

The ex-slaves was told that they would got things, different things. I don't know what all. I know they didn't got nothing and when freedom came they took their clothes and left. They scattered out and went to different places. It was hard to get work and there was no money cept what the Yankees give em. When they all got run off there was no money.

My husband was a Yankee soldier and he decided he wanter come to this country. We come on the train and on the boat to Pine Bluff. We farmed. I got three children but just two living. One boy lives at Fargo and the girl lives at Chicago. My husband died. Me and my sister lives here. I bought a place with my pension money. That since my husband died.

The present times is hard. I don't know nithin about these young folks. I tends to my own business. I ain't got nothing to do with the young folks. I don't know what causes the times to be so hard. Folks used to wear more clothes than they do and let colored folks have more ironing and bigger washings too. The washings bout played out. Some few folks hire cooks.

I farmed and washed and ironed and I have cooked along some here in Brinkley.

I am supported by my pension my husband left me. It ain't much but I make out with it. It is Union Soldiers Pension.

[HW: Hot Springs]

## Interviewer: Mary D. Hudgins
## Person interviewed: Anna Woods, 426 Grand Avenue

"Yes ma'am. Come on in. Is you taking lists of folks for old age pensions? Can you tell us what we going to get and when it's going to come? No? Then—Oh, I see you is writing us up. Well maybe that will help us to get attention. Cause we sure does need the pension.

To be sure I remembers slave days. My grandmother—she was give away in the trading yard. She was aflicted. What was the matter with her? Was she lame? No ma'am, she had the scrofula. So her mother was sold away from her, but she was give away. She was give away to a woman named Glover.

Mrs. Glover was a old woman when I knowed her. She was an old, old woman. She sort of studied before she'd say anything. She was a pretty good old woman though, Mrs. Glover was. She wouldn't let her colored folks be whipped. She wouldn't let me work in the field. Old Donovan wanted me to work in the field— but she wouldn't let him make me. Donovan was Mary's husband. Mary was Mrs. Glover's girl's girl. Mrs. Glover's girl was named Kate.

Mrs. Glover had a whole flock of slaves. My mother and another woman named Sallie cooked and did the washing. Fannie, she was my sister, was old Mrs. Glover's maid. Robert and Sally and Lucy—they was my brother and sisters—all of them worked in the field. They had to begin early and work late. They got them out way fore day. They worked them til dark.

I remembers that Sally and Lucy used to wear boots and roll their skirts up nearly to their waistses. Why—well you see sometimes it was muddy. Did we raise rice—No, ma'am. We mostly raised corn and cotton, like everybody else.

We lived near Natchez. No ma'am, I never see but one colored person whipped. His name was Robert. They laid him down on his stomach to whip him. Never did hear what he had done. Maybe he run off. They usually whipped them for that. No ma'am. I was right. Mrs. Glover didn't let her colored folks be whipped. Robert, you see, was Donovan's man. He didn't belong to Mrs. Glover. Her folks never got whipped.

Maybe Robert run off. I don't know. The folks did one thing special to keep them from running. They fastened a sort of yoke around they necks. From it there run up a sort of piece and there was a bell on the top of that. It was so high the folks who wore it couldn't reach the bell. But if they run it would tinkle and folks could find them. I don't quite know how it worked—I just slightly remembers.

No, ma'am, I was just sort of a little girl before the war. You might say I was never a slave. Cause I didn't have to work. Mrs. Glover wouldn't let me work in the field and I didn't have much work to do in the house either. Mrs. Glover was an old widow woman, but she was shore good. Miss Kate was her onliest child. Kate's daughter was named Mary.

Was I afraid of the soldiers? No ma'am. I wasn't.

Lots of them that came through were colored soldiers. I remember that they wore long tailed coats. They had brass buttons on they coats. But we had to move from Natchez.

First the soldiers run us off to Tennisaw Parish—an island there." (A check on maps in the atlas of Encyclopedia Britannica reveals a Tenses Parish, Louisiana—across the river and a few miles north of Natchez.) "We couldn't even stay there. They drove us along, and finally we wound up in Texas.

We wasn't there in Texas long when the soldiers marched in to tell us that we was free. Seems to me like it was on a Monday morning when they come in. Yes, it was a Monday. They went out to the field and told them they was free. Marched them out of the fields. They come a'shouting. I remembers one woman, she jumped up on a barrell and she shouted. She jumped off and she shouted. She jumped back on again and shouted some more. She kept that up for a long time, just jumping on a barrell and back off again.

190

Yes ma'am, we children played. I remembers that the grown folks used to have church—out behind an old shed. They'd shout and they'd sing. We children didn't know what it all meant. But every Monday morning we'd get up and make a play house in an old wagon bed—and we'd shout and sing too. We didn't know what it meant, or what we was supposed to be doing. We just aped our elders.

When the war was over my brother, he drove the carriage, he drove the white folks back to Natchez. But we didn't go—my family. We stopped part way to Natchez. Never did see Miss Kate or Mrs. Glover again. Never did see them again. Lots later my brother learned where we was. He came back for us and took us to Natchez. But we never did see Mrs. Glover again.

I lived on in Natchez. I worked for white folks—cooked for them. I did a lot of traveling. Even went up into Virginia. Traveled most of the time. I'd go with one family and when we'd get back, there'd be another one who wanted me to go and take care of their children.

Been in Hot Springs since 1905. Worked for Dr. ---- first. Stayed right in the house. Never did see such fine folks as Dr. ---- " (prominent local surgeon) "and his wife. Then I worked for Mr. ---- " (prominent realtor) "Yes, and I's worked at the Army and Navy Hospital too. Mighty nice up there. Worked in the officer's mess—finest place up there. I's worked for the officers too. Then I's worked for the Levi Hospital. Worked for lots of folks.

I's worked for lots of folks and in lots of places. But I haven't got anything now. How soon do you think they will begin paying us? I get just $10 from the county every month. $5 of that goes for my house. Folks gives me clothes, but if they'd only give me groceries too, I could get along. When do you think they will begin to pay us?

---

**Interviewer: Miss Irene Robertson**
**Person interviewed: Cal Woods; R.F.D., Biscoe, Arkansas**
**Age: 85?**

"I don't know zactly how old I is. I was good size boy when the war come on. We all belonged to a man named John Woods. We lived in South Carolina during slavery. Slavery was prutty bad itself but the bad time come after the war. The land was hilly some red and some pore and sandy. Had to plough a mule or horse. Hard to make a living. Some folks was rich, had heap of slaves and some bout one family. Small farmer have 160 acres and one family of slaves. When a man had one or two slave families he treated em better an if he had a great big acreage and fifteen or twenty families. The white folks trained the black man and woman. If he have so many they didn't learn how to do but one or two things. Mas generally they all worked in the fields in the busy seasons and sometimes the white folks have to work out there too. Sometimes they get in debt and have to sell off some slave to pay the debt.

"Things seemed heap mo plentiful. Before the war folks wore fine clothes. They go to their nearest tradin point and sell cotton. They had fine silk clothes and fine knives and forks. They would buy a whole case o cheese at one time and a barrel of molasses. Folks eat more and worked harder than they do now.

"Some folks was mean to their slaves and some slaves mean. It is lack it is now, some folks good no matter what dey color, other folks bad. Black folks never knowed there was freedom till they was fighting and going to war. Some say they was fightin to save their slaves, some say the Union broke. The slave never been free since he come to dis world, didn't know nuthin bout freedom till they tole em bout it.

"I recollect bout the Ku Klux after the war. Some folks come over the country and tell you you free and equal now. They tell you what to do an how to run the country and then if you listen to them come the Ku Klux all dressed half mile down the road. That Ku Klux sprung up after the war bout votin an offis-holdin mong the white folks. The white folks ain't then nor now havin no black man rulin over him. Them Ku Klux walked bout on high sticks and drink all the water you have from the spring. Seem lack they meddled a whole heap. Course the black folks knowed they was white men. They hung some slaves and white Yankees too if they be very mean. They beat em. Hear em hollowing and they hollow too. They shoot all directions round and up an down the road. That's how you know they comin close to yo house. If you go to any gatherins they come break it up an run you home fast as you could run and set the dogs on you. Course the dogs bite you. They say they was not goiner have equalization if they have to kill all the Yankees and niggers in the country. The masters sometime give em a home. My mother left John Woods then. The family went back. He give her an my papa twenty acres their lifetime. Where dey stayed on the old folks had a little at some places. They didn't divide up no plantations I ever heard of. They never give em no mules. If some tole em they would I know they sho didn't. Didn't give em nuthin I tell you. My mother's name was Sylvia and papa's name was Hack Woods.

"I come to Arkansas so my little boys would have a home. I had a little home an sold it to come out here. Agents come round showin pictures how big the cotton grow. They say it grow like trees out here. The children climb the stalks an set on the limb lack birds to pick it. They show pictures like that. Cotton basket way down under it on the ground. See droves of wild hogs coming up, look big as mules. Men ridin em. No I didn't know they said it was so fine. We come in freight cars wid our furniture and everything we brought. We had our provision in baskets and big buckets. It lasted till we passed Atlanta. We nearly starved the rest of the way. When we did stop you never hear such a hollein. We come two days and nights hard as we could come. We stayed up and eat, cooked meat an eggs on the stove in the store till daybreak. Then they showed us wha to go to our places the next day. I been here ever since.

"I hab voted. I done quit lettin votin bother me up. All I see it do is give one fellow out of two or three a job both of them maybe ought to have. The meanest man often gets lected. It the money they all after not the work in it. I heard em say what all they do and when they got lected they forgot to do all they say they would do.

"I never knowed bout no slave uprisins. Thed had to uprose wid rocks an red clods. The black man couldn't shoot. He had no guns. They had so much work they didn't know how to have a uprisin. The better you be to your master the better he treat you. The white preachers teach that in the church."

**Interviewer: Miss Irene Robertson**
**Person interviewed: Maggie Woods**
**Brassfield, Ark.**
**Deaner Farm.**
**Age: 70**

"My parents was Fannie and Alfred Douglas. They had three children, then he died and my mother married a man name Thompson. My parents belong to the Douglasses at Summerville, Tennessee. They had six children in their family.

"I was born the second year of the surrender that make me seventy years old. My folks was all field hands. They was all pure African stock. All black folks like me. Grandma Liney Douglass said she was sold and Grandpa was sold too. My own parents never was sold. The Douglass men-folks whooped the slaves but they was good masters outside of that.

"They would steal off and have preachin' at night. Had preachin' nearly all night sometimes. They'd hurry and get in home fore the day be breakin'. From the way they talked they done more prayin' than preachin'.

"Whenever they be sick they would send to the Douglasses to know what to do. They would take them up to their house and doctor them or come down to the quarters and wait on whoever be sick. They had some white doctors about but not near enough. They trained black women to be midwives.

"I think my folks had enough to eat and clothes too I recken. They eat meat to give them strength to work. My old stepdaddy always make us eat piece of meat if we eat garden stuff. He say the meat have strength in it. Cornbread, meat, peas and potatoes used to be the biggest part of folks livin' in olden days. They had plenty milk.

"Children when I come on didn't have no use for money. We eat molasses. Had a little candy once in a while. That be the best thing Santa Claus would bring me. We get ginger cakes in our new stockings too. Santa Claus been comin' ever since I been in the world. Seem like Christmas never would come round agin. It don't seem near so long now.

"I was too young to know about freedom. We was livin' on Douglas farm when George Flenol (white) come and brought us to Indian Bay. We worked on Dick Mayo's place. I don't know what they expected from freedom but I'm pretty sure they never got nothing.

"When the black folks come free then the Ku Klux took it up and made 'em work and stay at home. I heard that some folks wanted to stay in the road all the time. The Ku Klux nearly scared me to death to see pass by. They never did bother us.

"I don't vote. Don't know nothing about it. I don't like the way that is fixed for us to live now. We pay house rent and works as day laborers. It makes the work too heavy at some times and no work to do nearly all the time. It is making times hard. Cotton and corn choppin' time and cotton pickin' time is all the times a woman like me can work. I raised a shoat. I got no room for garden and chickens.

"I got one girl, she way from here, she sent me $2.00 for my Christmas.

"The young generation is weaker in body than us old folks has been. They ain't been raised to hard work and they don't hold out.

"That is salve I'm making. What do it smell like? It smell like chitlings. In that sack is the inside of the chitlings (hog manure). I boil it down and strain it, then boll it down, put camphor gum and fresh lard in it, boil it down low and pour it up. It is a green salve. It is fine for piles, rub your back for lumbago, and swab out your throat for sore throat. It is a good salve. I had a sore throat and a black woman told me how to make it. It cures the sore throat right now.

"I live on what I am able to work and make. I never have got no help from the government."

---

**Interviewer: Mrs. Bernice Bowden**
**Person interviewed: Sam Word, 1122 Missouri Street, Pine Bluff,**
**Arkansas**
**Age: 79**

"I'm a sure enough Arkansas man, born in Arkansas County near De Witt. Born February 14, 1859, and belonged to Bill Word. I know Marmaduke come down through Arkansas County and pressed Bill Word's son Tom into the service.

"I 'member one song they used to sing called the 'Bonnie Blue Flag.'

'Jeff Davis is our President
And Lincoln is a fool;
Jeff Davis rides a fine white horse
While Lincoln rides a mule.'

'Hurrah! Hurrah! for Southern rights,
Hurrah!
Hurrah for the Bonnie Blue Flag
That bears a Single Star!'"

(The above verse was sung to the tune of "The Bonnie Blue Flag." From the Library of Southern Literature I find the following notation about the original song and its author, Harry McCarthy: "Like Dixie, this famous song originated in the theater and first became popular in New Orleans. The tune was borrowed from 'The Irish Jaunting Car', a popular Hibernian air. Harry McCarthy was an Irishman who enlisted in the Confederate army from Arkansas. The song was written in 1861. It was published by A.E. Blackmar who declared General Ben Butler 'made it very profitable by fining every man, woman, or child who sang, whistled or played it on any instrument twenty-five dollars.' Blackmar was arrested, his music destroyed, and a fine of five hundred dollars imposed upon him.")

"I stayed in Arkansas County till 1866. I was about seven years old and we moved here to Jefferson County. Then my mother married again and we went to Conway County and lived a few years, and then I come back to Jefferson County, so I've lived in Jefferson County sixty-eight years.

"In Conway County when I was a small boy livin' on the Milton Powell place, I 'member they sent me out in the field to get some peaches about a half mile from the slave quarters. It was about three o'clock, late summer, and I saw something in the tree—a black lookin' concern. Seem like it got bigger the closer I got, and then just disappeared all of a sudden and I didn't see it go. I know I went back without any peaches.

"And another thing I can tell you. In the spring of the year we was hoein' and when they quit at night they'd leave the hoes in the field, stickin' down in the ground. And next morning they wouldn't be where you left 'em. You'd have to look for 'em and they'd be lyin' on top of the ground and crossed just like sticks.

"I'll tell you what I do know. When we was livin' in Conway County old man Powell had about ten colored families he had emigrated from Jefferson County. Our folks was the only colored people in that neighborhood. And he had a white man that was a tenant on the place and he died. Now my mother and his wife used to visit one another. In them days the white folks wasn't like they are now. And so mother went there to sit up with his wife. And while she was sittin' up the house was full of people—white and colored. They begin to hear a noise about the coffin. So they begin to investigate the worse it got and moved around the room and it lasted till he was took out of the house. Now I've heard white and colored say that was true. They never did see it but they heard it.

"I don't think there is any ghosts now but they was in the past generation.

"I know many times me and my stepfather would be pickin' cotton and my dog would be up at the far end of the row and just before dark he'd start barkin' and come towards us a barkin' and we never could see anything. He'd do that every day. It was a dog named Natch—an English bull terrier. He was give to me a puppy. He was a sure enough bulldog and he could whip any dog I ever saw. He was an imported dog.

"I remember a house up in Conway County made out of logs—a two-story one just this side of Cadron Creek on the Military Road. Then they called it the Wire Road because the telegraph wire run along it. The house was vacant after the people that owned it had died, and people comin' along late at night would stop to spend the night, and in the middle of the night they'd have to get out. Now I've heard that with my own ears. There was a spring not far from the house. It had been a fine house and was a beautiful place to stop. But in the night they'd hear chairs rattlin' and fall down. It's my belief they had spooks in them old days.

"Now I'll tell you another incident. This was in slave times. My mother was a great hand for nice quilts. There was a white lady had died and they were goin' to have a sale. Now this is true stuff. They had the sale and mother went and bought two quilts. And let me tell you, we couldn't sleep under 'em. What happened? Well, they'd pinch your toes till you couldn't stand it. I was just a boy and I was sleepin' with my mother when it happened. Now that's straight stuff. What do I think was the cause? Well, I think that white lady didn't want no nigger to have them quilts. I don't know what mother did with 'em, but that white lady just wouldn't let her have 'em.

"Now I'm puttin' the oil out of the can—I mean that what I say is true. People now will say they ain't nothin' to that story. At that time the races wasn't 'malgamated. But people are different now—ain't like they was seventy-five years ago.

"Visions? Well, now I'm glad you asked me that. I'll take pleasure in tellin' you. Two years before I moved to this place I had a vision and I think I saw every colored person that was ever born in America, I believe. I was on the east side of my house and this multitude of people was about four feet from me and they was as thick as sardines in a box and they was from little tots up. Some had on derby hats and some was bareheaded. I talked with one woman—a brown skinned woman. They was sitting on seats just like circus seats just as far as my eyes could behold. Looked like they reached clear up in the sky. That was when I fust went blind. You've read about how John saw the multitude a hundred forty and four thousand and I think that was about one-fourth of what I saw. They was happy and talkin' and nothin' but colored people—no white people.

"Another vision I had. I dreamed that the day that I lived to be sixty-five, that day I would surely die. I thought the man that told me that was a little old dried-up white man up in the air and he had scales like the monkey and the cat weighed the cheese. I thought he said, 'That day you will surely die,' and one side of the scales tipped just a little and then I woke up. You know I believed this strong. That was in 1919 and I went out and bought a lot in Bellwood Cemetery. But I'm still livin'.

"Old Major Crawley who owned what they called the Reader place on this side of the river, four miles east of Dexter, he was supposed to have money buried on his place. He owned it during slavery and after he died his relatives from Mississippi come here and hired a carriage driver named Jackson Jones. He married my second cousin. And he took 'em up there to dig for the money, but I don't know if they ever found it. Some people said the place was ha'nted."

199

**Interviewer: Mrs. Bernice Bowden**
**Person interviewed: Sam Word**
**1122 Missouri, Pine Bluff, Arkansas**
**Age: 78**

[TR: Same birthdate as previous informant.]

"I was born February 14, 1859. My birthplace was Arkansas County. Born in Arkansas and lived in Arkansas seventy-eight years. I've kept up with my age—didn't raise it none, didn't lower it none.

"I can remember all about the war, my memory's been good. Old man Bill Word, that was my old master, had a son named Tom Word and long about in '63 a general come and pressed him into the Civil War. I saw the Blue and the Gray and the gray clothes had buttons that said C.S., that meant secessioners. Yankees had U.S. on their buttons. Some of em come there so regular they got familiar with me. Yankees come and wanted to hang old master cause he wouldn't tell where the money was. They tied his hands behind him and had a rope around his neck. Now this is the straight goods. I was just a boy and I was cryin' cause I didn't want em to hang old master. A Yankee lieutenant comes up and made em quit—they was just the privates you know.

"My old master drove a ox wagon to the gold fields in California in '49. That's what they told me   that was fore I was born.

"Good? Ben Word good? My God Amighty, I wish I had one-hundredth part of what I got then. I didn't exist—I lived.

"Ben Word bought my mother from Phil Ford up in Kentucky. She was the housekeeper after old mistress died. I'll tell you something that may be amusing.

Mother had lots of nice things, quilts and things, and kept em in a chest in her little old shack. One day a Yankee soldier climbed in the back window and took some of the quilts. He rolled em up and was walking out of the yard when mother saw him and said, 'Why you nasty, stinkin' rascal. You may you come down here to fight for the niggers, and now you're stealin' from em.' He said, 'You're a G-D—liar, I'm fightin' for $14 a month and the Union.'

"I member there was a young man named Dan Brown and they called him Red Fox. He'd slip up on the Yankees and shoot em, so the Yankees was always lookin' for him. He used to go over to Dr. Allen's to get a shave and his wife would sit on the front porch and watch for the Yankees. One day the Yankees slipped up in the back and his wife said, 'Lord, Dan, there's the Yankees.' Course he run and they shot him. One of the Yankees was tryin' to help him up and he said, 'Don't you touch me, call Dr. Allen.' Yes ma'm, that was in Arkansas County.

"I never been anywhere 'cept Arkansas, Jefferson, and Conway Counties. I was in Conway County when they went to the precinct to vote for or against the Fort Smith & Little Rock Railroad. The precinct where they went to vote was Springfield. It used to be the county seat of Conway County.

"While the war was goin' on and when young Tom Word would come home from school, he learned me and when the war ended, I could read in McGuffy's Third Reader. After that I went to school three months for about four years.

"Directly after Emancipation, the white men in the South had to take the Oath of Allegiance. Old master took it but he hated to do it. Now these are stubborn facts I'm givin' you but they's true.

"After freedom mother brought me here to Pine Bluff and put me in the field. I picked up corn stalks and brush and carried water to the hands. Children in them days worked. After they come from school, even the white children had work to do. Trouble with the colored folks now, to my way of thinkin', is they are top heavy with literary learning and feather light with common sense and domestic training.

"I remember a song they used to sing daring the war:

'Jeff Davis is our President
Lincoln is a fool;
Jeff Davis rides a fine white horse
While Lincoln rides a mule.'

"And here's another one:

'Hurrah for Southern rights, hurrah!
Hurrah for the Bonny Blue Flag
That bore the single star.'

"Yes, they was hants sixty years ago. The generation they was interested has bred em out. Ain't none now.

"I never did care much for politics, but I've always been for the South. I love the Southland. Only thing I don't like is they don't give a square deal when it comes between the colored and the Whites. Ten years ago, I was worth $15,000 and now I'm not worth fifteen cents. The real estate men got the best of me. I've been blind now for four years and all my wife and I have is what we get from the Welfare."

---

**Interviewer: Mrs. Bernice Bowden**
**Person interviewed: Ike Worthy**
**2413 W. 11th Avenue, Pine Bluff, Arkansas**
**Age: 74**

"I was born in Selma, Alabama on Christmas day and I'm goin' on 75.

"I can 'member old missis' name Miss Liza Ann Bussey. I never will forget her name. Fed us in a trough—eighteen of us. Her husband was named Jim Bussey, but they all dead now.

"When I got large enough to remember we went to Louisiana. I was sixteen when we left Alabama—six hundred head of us. Dr. Bonner emigrated us there for hisself and other white men.

"There was nine of us boys in my parents' family. We worked every day and cleared land till twelve o'clock at night. On Saturday we played ball and on Sunday we went to Sunday school.

"We worked on the shares—got half—and in the fall we paid our debts. Sometimes we had as much as $150 in the clear.

"Most money I ever had was farmin'. I farmed 52 years and never did buy no feed. Raised my own meat and lard and molasses. Had four milk cows and fifteen to twenty hogs. You see, I had eight children in the family.

"Never went to school but one day in my life, then my father put us to work. Never learned to read. You see everybody in the pen now'days got a education. I don't think too much education is good for 'em.

"I was 74 Christmas day.

"Garland, Brewster—the sheriff and the judge—I missed them boys when they was little. Worked at the brickyard.

"I got shot accidental and lost my right leg 32 years ago when I was farmin'. I've chopped cotton and picked cotton with this peg-leg. Mr. Emory say he don't see how I can do it but I goes right along. I made $21 pickin' and $18 choppin' last year. I picked up until Thanksgiving night.

"I worked at the Long-Bell Lumber Company since I had this peg-leg too. I stayed in Little Rock 23 years. Had a wood yard and hauled wood.

"Yes ma'am, I voted the 'Publican ticket. No ma'am, I never did hold any office.

"I don't know what goin' come of the younger generation. To my idea I don't think there's anything to 'em. They is goin' to suffer when all the old ones is dead.

"I goes to the Zion Methodist Church. No ma'am, I'm not a preacher—just a bench member.

---

**Interviewer: Samuel S. Taylor**
**Person interviewed: Alice Wright**
**2418 Center Street, Little Rock, Arkansas**
**Age: About 74**

"I was born way yonder in slavery time. I don't know what part of Alabama nor exactly when, but I was born in slavery time and it was in Alabama. My oldest boy would be fifty-six years old if he were living. My father said he was born in slavery time and that I was born in slavery time. I was a baby, my papa said, when he ran off from his old master and went to Mississippi. He lived in the thickets for a year to keep his old master from finding out where he was.

**Father, Mother and Family**

"My father's name was Jeff Williams. He's been dead a long time. Nobody living but me and my children. My mother's name was Malinda Williams. My father had seven children, four girls and five boys. Four of the boys were buried on the Cummins (?) place. It used to be the old place of old Man Flournoy's. My oldest brother was named Isaac.

"I had sixteen children; four of them are still living—two boys and two girls. The boys is married and the daughters is sick. No, honey, I can't tell how many of em all was boys and girls.

204

## House

"My folks lived right in the white folks' yard. I don't know what kind of house it was. My mother used to cook and do for the white folks. She caught her death of cold going backward and forward milking and so on.

## How the Children were Fed

"They'd put a trough on the floor with wooden spoons and as many children as could get around that trough got there and eat, they would.

## How Freedom Came

"Dolly and Evelyn were upstairs spinning thread and overheard the old master saying that peace was declared but they didn't want the niggers to know it. Father had them to throw their clothes out the windows. Then he slipped out with them. Malinda Williams, my mother, came with them. Dolly and Evelyn were my sisters. I don't know my master's name, but it must have been Williams because all the slaves took their old master's names when they were freed. I was a baby in my daddy's arms when he ran away.

## Patrollers

"I heard my papa talk about the patrollers. He said they used to run them in many a time. That is the reason he had to cross the bridge that night going over the Mississippi into Georgia. The slaves had been set free in Georgia, and he wanted to get there from Alabama.

## What the Slaves Got

"The slaves never got nothin' when they were freed. They just got out and went to work for themselves.

## Marriage

"My father tended to the white folks' mules. He wasn't no soldier. When he married my mother, he was only fifteen years old. His master told him to go pick himself out a wife from a drove of slaves that were passing through, and he picked out my mother. They married by stepping over the broom. The old master pronounced them master and wife.

## Slave Droves

"The drove passed through Alabama, but my father didn't know where it came from nor where it went. They were selling slaves. They would pick up a big lot of them somewhere, and they would drive them across the country selling some every place they stopped. My master bought my mother out of the drove. Droves came through very often. I don't know where they came from.

## War Memories

"My father remembered coming through Alabama. He remembered the soldiers coming through Alabama. They didn't bother any colored people but they killed a lot of white people, tore up the town and took some white babies out and busted their brains out. That is what my father said. My father died in 1910. He was pushing eighty then and maybe ninety. He had a house full of grown children and grandchildren and great grandchildren. He wasn't able to do no work when he died. It was during the War that my father ran away into Georgia with me, too.

## Breeding

"My father said they put medicine in the water (cisterns) to make the young slaves have more children. If his old master had a good breeding woman he wouldn't sell her. He would keep her for himself.

## Worship

"When they were praying for peace they used to turn down the wash kettles to keep the sound down. In the master's church, the biggest thing that was preached to them was how to serve their master and mississ.

## Indians

"My grandmother was a full-blood Indian. I don't know from what tribe.

## Buried Treasure

"People used to bury their money in iron pots and chests and things in order to keep the soldiers from getting it. In Wabbaseka [HW: Ark.] there they had money buried. They buried their money to keep the soldiers from getting it.

## Ku Klux

"The Ku Klux Klan came after freedom. They used to take the people out and whip them.

## Just After the War

"Immediately after the War, papa farmed. Most of it was down at the Cummins place. When he ran away to Georgia, he didn't stay there. He left and came back to Mississippi. I don't know just when my papa came to the Cummins' place. It was just after the War. After be left the Cummins' place he worked at the Smith place. Then he was farming agent for sometime for old man Cook in Jefferson County. He would see after the hands.

## Voting

"I ain't never voted in my life. I know plenty men that used to vote but I didn't. I never heard of no women voting.

## Occupation

"I used to do field work. I washed and ironed until I got too old to do anything. I can't do anything now. I ain't able.

## Support

"I get the old age pension and the Welfare give me some commodities for myself and my sick daughter. She ain't been able to walk for a year.

## Marriage

"I married Willis Wright in July 1901. He did farming mostly. When he died in 1928, he was working at the Southern Oil Mill. He didn't leave any property."

**Interviewer: Mrs. Bernice Bowden**
**Person interviewed: Hannah Brooks Wright**
**W. 17th, Highland Addition, Pine Bluff, Arkansas**
**Age: 85**
**Occupation: Laundress**

"Yes ma'am, I was born in slavery times. I was born on Elsa Brooks' plantation in Mississippi. I don't know what year 'twas but I know 'twas in slavery times.

"I was a great big gal when the Yankees come through. I was Elsa Brooks' house gal.

"I remember when a man come through to 'vascinate' all the chillun that was born in slavery times. I cut up worse than any of 'em—I bit him. I thought he was gwine cut off my arm. Old missis say our names gwine be sent to the White House. Old missis was gwine around with him tryin' to calm 'em down.

"And the next day the Yankees come through. The Lord have mercy! I think I was 'bout twelve years old when freedom come. We used to ask old missis how old we was. She'd say, 'Go on, if I tell you how old you is, your parents couldn't do nothin' with you. Jus' tell folks you was born in slavery times!' Gramma wouldn't tell me neither. She'd say, 'You hush, you wouldn't work if you knowed how old you is.'

"I used to sit on the lever a many a day and drive the mule at the gin. You don't know anything 'bout that, do you?

"I remember one time when the Yankees was comin' through. I was up on top of a rail fence so I could see better. I said, 'Just look a there at them bluebirds.' When the Yankees come along one of 'em said, 'You get down from there you little son of a b----.' I didn't wait to climb down, I jus' fell down from there. Old missis come down to the quarters in her carriage—didn't have buggies in them days, just carriages—to see who was hurt. The Yankees had done told her that one of her gals had fell off the fence and got hurt. I said, 'I ain't hurt but I thought them Yankees would hurt me.' She said, 'They won't hurt you, they is comin' through to tell you you is free.' She said if they had hurt me she would jus' about done them Yankees up. She said Jeff Davis had done give up his seat and we was free.

"Our folks stayed with old missis as long as they lived. My mammy cooked and I stayed in the house with missis and churned and cleaned up. Old master was named Tom Brooks and her name was Elsa Brooks. Sometimes I jus' called her 'missis.'

"Old missis told the patrollers they couldn't come on her place and interfere with her hands. I don't know how many hands they had but I know they had a heap of 'em.

"Sometimes missis would say it looked like I wanted to get away and she'd say, 'Why, Hannah, you don't suffer for a thing. You stay right here at the house with me and you have plenty to eat.'

"I was the oldest one in my mammy's family.

"I just went to school a week and mammy said they needed me at the house.

"Then my daddy put me in the field to plow. Old missis come out one day and say, 'Bill, how come you got Hannah plowin'? I don't like to see her in the field.' He'd say, 'Well, I want to learn her to work. I ain't gwine be here always and I want her to know how to work.'

"They had me throwin' the shickles (shuttles) in slavery times. I used to handle the cyards (cards) too. Then I used to help clean up the milk dairy. I'd be so tired I wouldn't know what to do. Old missis would say, 'Well, Hannah, that's your job.'

"We used to have plenty to eat, pies and cakes and custards. More than we got now.

"I own this place if I can keep payin' the taxes.

"Old missis used to say, 'You gwine think about what I'm tellin' you after I'm dead and gone.'

"Young folks call us old church folks 'old *ism* folks,' 'old fogies.' They say, 'You was born in slavery times, you don't know nothin.' You can't tell 'em nothin'.

"I follows my mind. You ain't gwine go wrong if you does what your mind tells you."

**Interviewer: Miss Irene Robertson**
**Person interviewed: Tom Yates, Marianna. Arkansas**
**Age: 66**

"I was born in 1872 in Mississippi, on Moon Lake. Mama said she was orphan. She was sold when she was a young woman. She said she come from Richmond, Virginia to Charleston, South Carolina. Then she was brought to Mississippi and married before freedom. She had two husbands. Her owners was Master Atwood and Master Curtis Burk. I don't know how it come about nor which one bought her. She had four children and I'm the youngest. My sister lives in Memphis.

"My father was sold in Raleigh, North Carolina. His master was Tom Yeates. I'm named fer some of them. Papa's name was William Yeates. He told us how he come to be sold. He said they was fixing to sell grandma. He was one of the biggest children and he ask his mother to sell him and let grandma raise the children. She wanted to stay with the little ones. He said he cried and cried long after they brought him away. They all cried when he was sold, he said. I don't know who bought him. He must have left soon after he was sold, for he was a soldier. He run away and want in the War. He was a private and mustered out at DeValls Bluff, Arkansas. That is how come my mother to come here. He died in 1912 at Wilson, Arkansas. He got a federal pension, thirty-six dollars, every three months. He wasn't wounded, or if he was I didn't hear him speak of it. He didn't praise war."

**Interviewer: Mrs. Bernice Bowden**
**Person interviewed: Annie Young, 913 West Scull Street,**
    **Pine Bluff, Arkansas**
**Age: 76**

"My old master's name was Sam Knox. I 'members all my white people. My mother was the cook.

"We had a good master and a good mistress too. I wish I could find some of my master's family now. But after the war they broke up and went up North.

"I 'member well the day my old master's son got killed. My mother was workin' in the field and I know she come to the house a cryin'. I 'member well when we was out in the plum nursery and could hear the cannons. My white girl Nannie told me 'Now listen, that's the war a fightin'.'

"The soldiers used to come along and sometimes they were in a hurry and would grab something to eat and go on and then sometimes they would sit down to a long table.

"I could hear my great grandmother and my mother talkin' 'We'll be free after awhile.'

"After the war my stepfather come and got my mother and we moved out in the piney woods. My stepfather was a preacher and sometimes he was a hundred miles from home. My mother hired out to work by the day. I was the oldest of seven chillun and when I got big enough to work they worked me in the field. When we cleaned up the new ground we got fifty cents a day.

"I was between ten and twelve years old when I went to school. My first teacher was white. But I tell you the truth, I learned most after my children started to school.

"I worked twenty-three years for the police headquarters. I was janitor and matron too. I washed and ironed too. I been here in Pine Bluff about fifty or sixty years.

"If justice was done everybody would have a living. I earned the money to buy this place and they come and wanted me to sign away my home so I could get the old age pension but I just had sense enough not to do it. I'm not goin' sign away my home just for some meat and bread."

---

**Interviewer: Mrs. Bernice Bowden**
**Person interviewed: John Young**
**925 E. 15th Ave., Pine Bluff, Ark.**
**Age: 92**

"Well, I don't know how old I is. I was born in Virginia, but my mother was sold. She was bought by a speculator and brought here to Arkansas. She brought me with her and her old master's name was Ridgell. We lived down around Monticello. I was big enough to plow and chop cotton and drive a yoke of oxen and haul ten-foot rails.

"Oh Lord, I don't know how many acres old master had. He had a territory—he had a heap a land. I remember he had a big old carriage and the carriage man was Little Alfred. The reason they called him that was because there was another man on the place called Big Alfred. They won't no relation—just happen to be the same name.

"I remember when the Yankees come and killed old master's hogs and chickens and cooked 'em. There was a good big bunch of Yankees. They said they was fightin' to free the niggers. After that I runned away and come up here to Pine

Bluff and stayed awhile and then I went to Little Rock and jined the 57th colored infantry. I was the kittle drummer. We marched right in the center of the army. We went from Little Rock to Fort Smith. I never was in a big battle, just one little scrummage. I was at Fort Smith when they surrendered and I was mustered out at Leavenworth, Kansas.

"My grandfather went to war as bodyguard for his master, but I was with the Yankees.

"I remember when the Ku Klux come to my grandmother's house. They nearly scared us to death. I run and hid under the bed. They didn't do nothin', just the looks of 'em scared us. I know they had the old folks totin' water for 'em. Seemed like they couldn't get enough.

"After the war I come home and went to farmin'. Then I steamboated for four years. I was on the Kate Adams, but I quit just 'fore it burned, 'bout two or three weeks.

"I never went to school a minute in my life. I had a chance to go but I just didn't.

"No'm I can't remember nothin' else. It's been so long it done slipped my memory."

---

**Interviewer: Mrs. Bernice Bowden**
**Person interviewed: John Young**
**923 E. Fifteenth, Pine Bluff, Arkansas**
**Age: 89**

"I know I was born in Arkansas. The first place I recollect I was in Arkansas.

"I was a drummer in the Civil War. I played the little drum. The bass drummer was Rheuben Turner.

"I run off from home in Drew County. Five or six of us run off here to Pine Bluff. We heard if we could get with the Yankees we'd be free, so we run off here to Pine Bluff and got with some Yankee soldiers—the twenty-eighth Wisconsin.

"Then we went to Little Rock and I j'ined the fifty-seventh colored infantry. I thought I was good and safe then.

"We went to Fort Smith from Little Rock and freedom come on us while we was between New Mexico and Fort Smith.

"They mustered us out at Fort Leavenworth and I went right back to my folks in Drew County, Monticello.

"I've been a farmer all my life till I got too old."

---

www.ingramcontent.com/pod-product-compliance
Lightning Source LLC
Chambersburg PA
CBHW080557030426
42336CB00019B/3220